1. 4

CALLING FOR ACTION

CALLING FOR ACTION

An Autobiographical Enquiry

Donald Soper

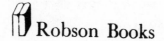 Robson Books

Acknowledgment I am indebted to my son-in-law Terence Blacker and his wife, my youngest daughter Caroline, for all the professional help they have provided in the preparation of this book.

FIRST PUBLISHED IN GREAT BRITAIN IN 1984 BY ROBSON BOOKS LTD., BOLSOVER HOUSE, 5–6 CLIPSTONE STREET, LONDON W1P 7EB. COPYRIGHT © 1984 DONALD SOPER.

British Library Cataloguing in Publication Data

Soper, Donald
 Calling for action.
 1. Christian life
 I. Title
 248.4   BV4501.2

 ISBN 0–86051–265–7

Typeset by Preface Ltd, Salisbury
Printed in Hungary

None should know better than a parson how carefully the word 'dedication' should be used. I have no hesitation, however, in offering this book as a dedication to my wife Marie. Her love, her understanding and her tolerance have been both my safeguard and my inspiration for more than fifty years.

CONTENTS

INTRODUCTION

The man in the crowd was becoming increasingly restive. He expressed total disagreement with what I was trying to say about the Christian Gospel, declaring it to be a load of rubbish. Finally, he delivered his punchline: 'The trouble with you parsons is that you are all mad.'

Not unnaturally I disagreed with him, but he would have nothing of it and, as if to clinch the issue, he demanded: 'If you are not mad – prove it!'

I must say that I found such a challenge somewhat disconcerting. I had frequently been accused of being unreasonable, occasionally been labelled as an idiot, but never before had I been called upon to provide conclusive evidence of my sanity. So, hoping to play for time, I asked the heckler whether he could prove that *he* was not mad.

He said he could and he did, producing with a flourish his discharge certificate, as he called it, from a mental hospital. I was sensible enough in the merriment that greeted this sally to leave the Gospel, temporarily at least, for a more propitious occasion.

Later I thought about the heckler's accusation. What, in more technical language, is insanity? It is, surely, a condition in which what is going on in one's head is insulated from, or contrary to, what is going on all around it. If I live in a private world of my own which has nothing to do with the real world outside, I am mad. Insanity is disassociation and, in this sense, the heckler was, in his own intransigent way, calling attention to a very real problem for the Christian advocate.

Can it not be argued that Christianity, and more particularly the

Church, is an example of irrelevance bearing no genuine relationship to the world of actual experience? Is not going to church an excursion into a realm of wishful thinking and the longer your stay there, the more remote your isolation from what is actually going on?

This book is an attempt to examine that charge and to do so from a personal standpoint which can so easily be overlooked. After more than sixty years in the vocation of a practising Christian, I am no longer greatly disturbed by those who tell me that my activities in a Mission church or my weekly advocacy in the open air have been either unreasonable or, worse still, mentally afflicted. To run, or help to run, a hostel for young delinquents, to set up a centre for the rehabilitation of alcoholics, to organize a rest centre during air raids or a home for destitute old people, is not a piece of work 'cribbed and confined' in make-believe. This, surely, is the practical aspect of an effective Christian ministry. Whatever else happens at Speakers' Corner or on Tower Hill, one thing is certain: you are heard only if you are relevant. I have found in all this what St Paul called 'a reasonable service'. Looked at as an act of obedience, this ministry is self-rewarding both in its achievements and just as much in its failures. Although I continue to believe that the essence of Christianity is obedience, it is not possible to ignore the speculation as to its outcome.

The wages of going on depend to some extent on the future prospect of the 'firm' in which you are working. So, rejecting as I do the blatant accusation of that heckler, that Christianity is a way of life which is basically unreal, and finding myself unshaken by some of the more sophisticated criticisms of religion as a retreat from reality, there still remain important questions to be answered.

Is the hope, let alone the assurance, that the Christian Gospel will prevail and that the Kingdom of God is on the way a reasonable prospect? How does the promise of Peace on Earth and Goodwill Among Men with its association with Glory to God in the Highest sound after the two thousand years since first it was offered?

It must now surely be agreed that the issues of Peace and Goodwill are incomparably the most urgent and the most critical that face us. The nuclear age has introduced an apocalyptic dimension to the promise. Hitherto war has only possessed a limited capacity to destroy and, until now, Goodwill, however ardent, has been equally limited in its capability. Today they have acquired total competence: nuclear war could destroy the world itself, just as science has made possible the correction of all the economic and human causes of ill-will, potentially providing enough for each and enough for all.

Unlike the ancient shepherds who heard that first Christmas message, many people today would reject the requirements to quote 'Glory to God' as the precondition of the promise of Peace and Goodwill. This no longer appears a necessary relationship to many thinkers and the majority of organized communities.

I have preached many a sermon on the adventure of faith, that the would-be Christian is invited to build his life on Christ and His Kingdom, and I have no reason to disavow such an appeal. At the same time there lies at the heart of the Gospel promise as well as adventure, and the essence of a 'promise' is the capacity to deliver. Maybe I have concentrated on this adventure of walking by faith and not by sight because, unconsciously, I have found myself more at home in this aspect of the Christian life than in the certainty of its fulfilment. Pilgrimage is a word that appears time and time again; predestination hardly appears at all.

Now, at eighty-one, I am disposed in so many ways to take a deeper interest in ends rather than means. What is the end likely to be and how do the experiences of my own life bear upon this prospect? Were the answers only to be available in the next world, then patience is the required virtue. The moment, however, that the Kingdom of God is regarded in time as well as in eternity, the question becomes an absorbing one and, because I happen to be a creature of time, whatever may be my eternal condition, my experiences can be relevant to its answer.

This brings me to the title of my book, *Calling For Action*. It has an obvious, but I hope permissible *double entendre* where the author is a clergyman. The calling to which I am committed and dedicated, is of its nature an intellectual and theological attitude, but it also invites the believer to act in a particular way so as to express that creed. Moreover, the plain teaching of Jesus is that He is Lord, that is, He is to be obeyed. The would-be Christian is called to seek first the Kingdom of God; in fact to act as if it is already here: 'The Kingdom is amongst you', said Jesus. In that supreme sense, my calling is for action now.

The call for action in the second sense of those words is not confined to parsons. The calling is directed to everybody. It presents an unprecedented challenge in a political, religious and human group which, for the first time, can be a 'ministry of all the talents'. The democratic society not only offers rights to every member, but also it demands, if it is not going to wither, the cooperation of every voting member in order to prosper. Clergymen may have a particular kind of calling for action, but it must not be left to any one ministry, ecclesiastical or parliamentary. The present human condition requires the sending out of a 'general alert'.

As to the plan of action itself, the subject matter naturally falls under three heads, the three propositions in the Christian Gospel: Peace on Earth, Goodwill Among Men and Glory to God. Although at many points Peace and Goodwill and Glory to God overlap and intertwine, they can be approached separately and I will try to treat them one by one.

However, the quest for truth is always unprofitable unless it is pursued within the vital, untidy world that is the only real one. I therefore intend to treat the three proposals on the first Christmas Eve in a somewhat different order from that in which they were first couched. I do not doubt that the promises of Peace on Earth and Goodwill Among Men are contingent upon the belief in the God who ordains and therefore makes possible these blessings. Nonetheless, to set Peace and Goodwill in the context of events, and events in which I have been involved, falls naturally into the mould that I have outlined. I shall seek, therefore to locate these three issues in my own experiences and to introduce them as they have confronted me.

To that extent the book is autobiographical, but it is not intended as a personal diary and makes no attempt at the strict continuity of a personal chronicle.

I have long been fascinated by Marcel Proust and that inimitable masterpiece, *A la Recherche du Temps Perdu*. His famous recall of things past, of how their resurrection or reminiscence brings them to life and meaning again, is particularly relevant here. A certain event or experience, trivial in itself, opens the magic casement on to an otherwise forgotten and lost world. The mental recall of what happened brings with it the feel, aroma and immediacy which otherwise time destroys. Proust relives his childhood as he calls to mind the spoonful of tea in which has been dunked a morsel of madeleine cake. To live again the joy this simple reminiscence brought to him, is to defeat the ravages of time which otherwise would sweep the past into oblivion.

12

For me, to hear a particular melody, especially one which comes from hymns from Sunday School days, is to flesh out the dry bones of memory with the warmth and impact of all sorts of occasions when I heard and sang these hymns long ago. The power of recall is even more potent in the case of that other of our senses — smell. Wave a bar of Wright's Coal Tar soap under my nose and I am immediately in Minehead on holiday as a child, being lathered with that particular brand of soap after the train journey from London, during which I had understandably become grubby.

Whatever the conclusions Proust reached from the prosecution of the power of the emotions when focused on remembered incidents — and I confess that his concept of the eternity of art amid the corruption by time of all else leaves me unsure both of what he meant, and my own ability to understand it anyhow — they are certainly irreconcilable to the Christian Gospel. But for the present purpose I intend to borrow his method and, in my case, not only to preserve the past but also to anticipate the future.

To those who rightly insist that before you can look with optimism on the proclamation of the Heavenly Host you must first get to know what it is really like in order to advance its claims, I would offer a sample of incidents from the various fields of my ministry which serve to create or recreate the atmosphere in which that kind of advocacy takes place. It is an atmosphere which is dynamic, not only in the sense that a lot happens and much of it all at once, but also because it is personal rather than cerebral. It involves people, body and soul and spirit, thoughts, feelings, warts and all.

This is all the more significant in my case for, apart from eucharistic worship, in particular the celebration of Holy Communion, it is in the large and loud arena of the open air that I feel more confident about the future than anywhere else. So it is especially important that I should be able to capture the spirit of such occasions, and pass it on as best I can to the reader.

One way of doing this would be to present a *curriculum vitae* of this exercise — the familiar autobiographical procedure. Yet, in the retelling of the events, the spirit with which they were impregnated may be lost. Tower Hill, for example, comes alive for me as I catch the spirit of the crowd, its down-to-earth questioning, its particular brand of humour. Let me try to catch that humour with a typical expression of it.

The day was sunny and the crowd was involved in a more than

13

usually theological argument. There suddenly appeared, rushing towards me, an attractive young lady wearing a large flowered hat. It transpired that she was bent on delivering a writ on behalf of someone engaged in litigation with the Methodist Church. As President of the Conference that year, I was the suitable recipient of such a document and my whereabouts on Wednesdays were well known. Such was her errand, though her purpose as she edged her way towards me at that moment was undisclosed. Her approach was being followed with growing interest. Finally, as she handed me the writ, a voice from the back of the crowd yelled out: 'You ought to be ashamed of yourself, why don't you marry the girl?' The crowd at that moment might have belonged to a different species from that which had been engaged in the theological argument. Happily, the young lady was no more disturbed than I, but the whole atmosphere of the meeting was transformed.

This sort of human recollection tells more about truth and our awareness of it than a thousand academic statements. I think that is why my grandfather treasured *Three Men in a Boat* almost as much as his prayer book. He was a friend of Jerome K. Jerome's and also of George and Harris, and he often joined them in excursions up the River Thames. This immortal book was read to me when I was very young until I knew the story of Uncle Podger's picture hangings, George's battle with the swans and other of my grandfather's favourite passages off by heart.

This is the sort of humour which, more than anything else, demonstrates how volatile are the circumstances which surround activities like evangelism and how varied therefore is the reception given to what is said. I know how much more assured I am as to the credibility of the Gospel from time to time and from occasion to occasion and, strangely enough, it is the humorous occasions which live in my memory as among the most favourable. They would come in the cut and thrust of debate with the crowd, and the secret I have painfully acquired over the years is to try and make use of such occasions. Not that it always works that way. I remember the man who was expatiating on America.

'Have you ever been to America?' I asked. 'No.' came the reply. So I told him not to speak on matters he knew nothing about.

'Have you ever been to Heaven?' he retorted. I had, of course, to say 'No', and he delivered his *coup de grace*:

*'Then don't *you* speak on matters you know nothing about.'

The many moods of the crowd, from bird-mindedness to intensity, from laughter to anger, from obduracy to receptivity, have opened up for me the meaning of the unity of thought and action. Thought is neither pure nor isolatable from the circumstance in which it is formulated. The deeper the emotional setting, the more the argument is transformed with shifts of meaning which go far beyond rationality. Pascal's insistence that 'The heart has its reasons that reason itself cannot comprehend' appealed to me the very first time I read the *Pensées*. How strengthened and consolidated has been the impact of that aphorism as the years and the vicissitudes of a ministerial calling have gone by.

So much then for the frame of mind and heart which I bring to the specific matters proclaimed by the Heavenly Host two thousand years ago. I could almost take as the text of my confession of faith the words in the *Pensées* which follow his famous aphorism. Here is the gist of them:

> We know the truth not only through our reason but also through our heart. It is through the latter that we know first principles, and reason, which has nothing to do with it, tries in vain to refute them. The sceptics have no other object than that, and they work at it to no purpose. We know that we are not dreaming, but, however unable we may be to prove it rationally, our inability proves nothing but the weakness of our reason, and not the uncertainty of all our knowledge, as they maintain.

To this I can only say 'Amen'.

D. S., 1984

Part One

Peace on Earth

CHAPTER ONE

THE BOOK WAS *With the Flag to Pretoria;* its subject was the Boer War, which had just ended when I was born. Among the many photographs in it was an impressionist sketch of a British soldier on sentry-duty at night, out on the south African veld. Even now, after more than three-quarters of a century since I first saw that lonely sentry, the recollection of it takes me back irresistibly and immediately to my first impressions of the ominous silence of his vigil and the lurking dangers in that darkness. This vivid image opens the door to a room full of memories of the world in which I lived as a boy of eleven and of which I was beginning to take notice.

It was the year in which the First World War broke out. My younger brother Ross – whom we called Sos – my sister Millicent and I were holidaying with our parents at Heacham on the east coast when war was declared and, on that day, my father and I walked into the village to buy the morning paper. On the front page was a picture of the Kaiser in the uniform of the Death's Head Hussars. Later that night we heard the sound of guns out at sea. Concerned that we might be in danger of invasion where we were, my father decided that we should all immediately return to London.

At the time, my father was an average adjustor, that is to say he was an expert in marine insurance. But his leisure hours were committed to the work of the Church in which he was a kind of lay preacher. My mother was a teacher and was later to became a headmistress.

Once back at home, I was quickly involved in the war effort. The Methodist Sunday School, which was under the superintendency of my father, and which was a sort of second home to me was, like many another Sunday School throughout the country, to contribute to victory by putting on a patriotic pageant. The impact of this event was all the more significant because, for a boy in a Methodist household, Sunday School was the central activity of the Church. It took place on Sunday afternoon, and started with what was almost a replica of the Church service itself, being composed of prayers and hymns. After the service, we would forgather in classes to be instructed in the Christian faith, after which we would reassemble and sing some more hymns. We would then be dismissed in time for tea.

For my part in the pageant, I was dressed up as a French *poilu* and belted out the 'Marseillaise' at a performance, the rest of which I have completely forgotten. What I have not forgotten, however, is the total acceptance of the war as a 'righteous cause' and Kipling's recessional hymn, which we sang nearly as frequently as the National Anthem:

> *God of our fathers, known of old,*
> *Lord of our far-flung battle line,*
> *Beneath whose awful hand we hold*
> *Dominion over palm and pine —*
> *Lord God of Hosts, be with us yet,*
> *Lest we forget — lest we forget!*

On the more secular front I was very soon drafted into the school cadet corps, issued with a uniform and a wooden rifle, and required to polish brass buttons at least once a week as preparation for an afternoon of drill every Wednesday. Naturally enough, as time went by I began to relate to the war conditions in a less childish way.

My early years were couched in a particular environment of thought and assurance. I was born in London which I was persuaded was the greatest city in the world and, considering the areas of red on the world's map, I believed that I was a member of the greatest empire the world had known. Each Empire Day confirmed these ingrained assumptions and in the middle class to which my parents belonged, and in which they lived so much of their lives, I was insulated against the industrial and political turbulence which was convulsing human societies elsewhere. Of course, these dominant impressions had nothing to do with considered judgements dependent on satisfactory evidence – what they did was to reflect a climate of opinion more or less uncritically accepted and, in my eleven years, completely, inaccurately imbibed.

The main ingredient of that climate was the ozone of power. The lonely sentry was in personal danger but, whatever happened to him, the war to which he was exposed would inevitably be won. The peril only emphasized that overall triumph. *With the Flag to Pretoria* was a victory march by an unconquerable British Empire. The patriotic pageant at the Sunday School was not, in the eyes of those who promoted it, an unfortunate but necessary interruption of the hymns and prayers and lessons to which we were accustomed on Sunday afternoons. Instead, it was an obvious representation of the proper conduct of Christian activities, of what Sunday School should be about – the intimate relation between the power of God and the power of Britain. The pageant was as much a celebration of that power as it was a demonstration of loyal commitment to its preservation. My *poilu* was part of the pageant because the French were quite properly recognizing that power, and equally properly backing it up.

The same sense of power seemed to impregnate the cadet uniform which I put on when I came under the Wednesday command of the military officer who was my history master the rest of the week. The insignia on the cap linked me with a famous regiment and, although I never really mastered the winding of puttees, they reminded me of the far-flung empire wherein they first became the standard equipment of an unbeatable army. Whether or not this sense of indomitable might was shared by the community as a whole, I at least had no occasion to doubt it. Indeed, subsequent conversations with my contemporaries, some of whom came from differing backgrounds, tend to confirm the claim that such a *Weltanschauung* was pervasive throughout the whole country.

Nonetheless, it was a false assessment. The empire was in decline and the war itself both underlined and accelerated that decline. Economically, Germany had already overtaken us and politically, the USA had usurped our international role. The world called to mind by the Boer War sentry was an unreal one. The significance of the clusters of impressions and assumptions which it still conjures up lies not in their truth but in their prevalence. Man may make his own history but, as often as not, he makes it up and, whether he believes it or not, his children are likely to accept it. I did, and some residual effects of that early indoctrination remain to this day.

21

This climate of power which, however factitious, contributed to my first introduction to the supreme issue of war and peace was characterized by a moral element alongside the so-called factual one. The assumption of invulnerability was intertwined with a compounding assumption of moral rectitude. We not only won the Boer War, in the sense at least that the enemy could not maintain its military resistance, but there was no doubt that we would win the 'War to end Wars'. For these were the victories of right over wrong as well as the triumphs of superior ability. That sentry was not just in conflict with an adversary, he represented the struggle between good and evil. He was to be admired not only for his martial ability but more especially as the lonely champion of a just cause, enduring the hazards and dangers of life and death against evil men who were lurking in wait for him. It was this that I, along with millions of my fellow countrymen, believed.

In fact, if I had any doubts as to the moral justification for the war against the Dutch settlers, they disappeared when I read that the Boers were using dum-dum bullets which expanded on impact, as opposed to the morally justifiable British bullets which penetrated their victims in a straightforward and therefore morally justifiable manner.

In 1914, the Germans took the place of the Boers as the force of evil. The well-known picture of the Kaiser in the sinister head-dress of the Death's Head Hussars clearly proclaimed his obvious wickedness. Those hymns that we sang in Sunday School reinforced the need to send the King victorious as the National Anthem proclaimed. We knew it was God who had made us mighty and, if suitably petitioned, would make us mightier still. Kipling's hymn did warn us of the pride that might accompany victory but left no doubt as to the righteousness of the imperial cause. The war was a particular application of the Christian conscience. No one, as far as I was concerned, ecclesiastical or lay, suggested even the possibility to me that the power of conducting mass violence did not necessarily confer moral approval on its practice.

It is a melancholy fact that, while this country's power in the world has declined considerably since those imperial days, many of the attitudes and assumptions that were prevalent then are far from uncommon today. I suppose that 'jingoism' is the appropriate word. It is a term associated with a particular phase in our history and for a long time I was convinced that the frame of mind it represented, which was so much a part of my early years, would never reappear.
22

In fact, looking back, I am now quite certain that it never really did disappear, but was merely less visible.

The hold of nationalism on people's minds has diminished very little. As I write these words, I reflect particularly on the Falklands episode, or the Falklands disaster as I believe it will turn out to be. Like the Bourbons, it appears that we have forgotten nothing and learnt nothing and, however anachronistic the treaties and pretensions of imperialism now appear, the underlying emotions still persist alarmingly.

The link between the Falklands and the Boer War does not end there. Again, the Church failed in any way to repudiate this kind of sanctified jingoism. It is easy enough to criticize organized Christianity and I have no desire to wash its dirty linen in public. But at the same time I could have wished that over the years the attitude of Christianity in general, and the organized Churches in particular, to the whole question of armaments and peacemaking had been transformed by the experience not only of those earliest years in my lifetime but two world wars subsequently.

The fact is, however, that in many respects it has not, and indeed I detect a decay of the peacemaking ardour. At the present time there appears to be a perceptible decline in the fervour of the Church in respect of organized violence itself and, under the pressures particularly of resistance movements in the present world, I sense a tendency to draw back from the kind of reaction against warfare which was prompted by the events of the First World War and very largely supplemented by those of the Second.

I feel bound to add that the more I consider what the Church should do and should be in the world of today, the more convinced I become that there is a polarization between Church and State which is ultimately irreconcilable. My belief is that it is ultimately impossible for there to be a working relationship between the modern state and effective churchmanship, indeed that there are incompatibilities here which prevent not only an alliance but any kind of working agreement. A polarization between Church and State would, of course, pose immense problems, yet the truth is unavoidable. The kind of modern state which is self-sufficient, committed to certain violence and is a predatory as well as an unnatural coming together of human beings, could never be an expression of that Kingdom of God, in which the Christian ought to believe.

As I reflect now upon my baptism of fire those many years ago,

23

the most sinister aspect of it was the self-justifying of power and its expression in war. It was as if power itself was morally acceptable and its possession conferred on those who employed it an ethereal quality. The fact that I came quite early to question that identification of power and morals, I shall endeavour to treat in the following chapter.

CHAPTER TWO

THE NUMBERS 1 2 3   1 5 4 have an irresistible attraction for me. Whenever I think of them in that sequence, I am taken back to a series of events in my life, and in the world of my experience, which began in the years immediately following the 1918 armistice and which characterized my days as a university student at St Catharine's College, Cambridge, where I went to read History in 1921. The numbers represent, of all things, the various lethal methods of using a rifle with a bayonet stuck on its barrel. The first three are thrusts with the bayonet, the others blows with either the barrel or the butt of the rifle.

The year the First World War ended I began to train as a bayonet-fighting instructor in the cadet corps at Aske's School, Hatcham. I passed the army gymnastic staff examination with an essay on 'The Spirit of the Bayonet' which contained, as I remember, such helpful advice as the importance of grunting as you stick the bayonet in. I became entitled to wear a badge of crossed swords on my cap and, to begin with, it all seemed an entirely proper and exciting development from my earlier attitude to war and its requirements.

Without being a particularly blood-thirsty teenager, I remember enjoying my bayonet-fighting days in the school corps. For me, it was a splendid, if not actually heroic form of 'knightly prowess', involving skill, guts and spirit. Nonetheless, I can now appreciate that the bayonet-fighting episode was, in fact, the end of a personal era and the beginning of another, a time in which I began to question the hitherto uncriticized assumptions about the whole matter of war and mass violence. Aided and abetted by the

25

experience of leaving home for the first time and being confronted as a university student with the strange and demanding new world of the years immediately following the Treaty of Versailles, the experience of 'The Spirit of Bayonet' was a catalyst.

Perhaps the first seeds of unease and scepticism about 'The Spirit of the Bayonet' and all it represented, were sown by the Grenadier Guardsman who was my teacher. A giant of a man, he was instructing us school cadets because of war wounds which had left him with only half of one hand and a broken gait. On one occasion, I asked him whether he had practised in a real battle what 1 2 3   1 5 4 prescribed. He replied that he had not and that he would have been considerably more concerned to have a bullet in his rifle than a bayonet on the end of it.

When I went to Cambridge at the age of eighteen, I did not take with me my crossed swords. Instead, I took a cricket bat. Now a raw recruit rather than an instructor, I found myself mixing with a very different group of contemporaries. Most of them were much older and wiser than I. Naval captains and high-ranking soldiers had rooms on the same staircase where I 'kept'. I played cricket with men who bore the scars and sometimes the physical handicaps of war wounds. Bayonet-fighting instruction quickly faded into irrelevance as I began to hear at first-hand the realities of war.

The very reticence of those who spoke to me about it, was revealing. The so-called 'martial exercise' that I had enjoyed became part of an obscenity of which I was ashamed. Now my reaction to war was, I thought, based on reasonable grounds, but to what extent was the emotional wish father to the rational thought? I had been fortunate enough to escape the actual and deadly practice of bayonet-fighting, but the horror of it was all the greater because my imagination could play upon it, as it came to me through the experience of my elders and especially my soldier fellow students. Those emotions both fascinated and shocked me.

In particular, I remember meeting during a vacation the husband of one of the teachers at my mother's school. I can see him now, with a collapsed and useless lung and a look of resignation, and indeed of bewilderment, in his eyes, as I prised out of him something of what it had been like to rot in the trenches. I was terrified at the thought that what he had done and what had happened to him might happen to me. That fear must have concentrated my mind and it cannot be excluded from the dominant agents which contributed to my renunciation of war, and my confidence that such a renunciation could be universally successful. But if fear is a very good servant, it is an intolerable master. To recognize that fear can be the beginning of wisdom is as applicable to the thought of God as it is to the thought of war. When, however, it becomes, willy-nilly, the principal reaction to war, it is thoroughly untrustworthy. It may even become counter-productive. There is a morbid fascination about anything which promotes horror. Koestler's *Darkness at Noon* brilliantly explores this macabre territory wherein what are regarded as normal human responses 'go wild' when under powerful emotional stresses.

I would not pretend to have an expert understanding of such psychological matters but I will set down what I would argue is a sequence of the responses that fear and horror produce. First, there is the trauma induced by the mental experience of that horror. Second, there comes a process of rejection of that experience because it is so distressing as to become intolerable – we deliberately turn it out of our minds because to retain it is too painful. At the third stage, and here the trouble starts, we are able to persuade ourselves that the horror we have dismissed from our thoughts has been equally dismissed from reality. We do not think about it and it goes away. Of course, such a conclusion is a most dangerous fallacy.

But there were also rational elements behind this questioning mood, for that is all that it amounted to, in my first years at Cambridge. The first and the most important had to do with a belief, which so many of the returned warriors seemed to exude, that the world would never be the same again. It would never again demand the blood-letting of which they had been a part. I was reading for the History Tripos, and it seemed to me that, hitherto, this sort of optimism about the future was altogether too fragile, considering the repeated wars that had convulsed previous generations and, further, that whatever results and changes had followed previous wars, the war machine had itself never been dismantled.

Yet it could now, for the first time, be different. Here was an unprecedented opportunity to renounce war and its machinery. I shared with many others a confidence that the prospect of Peace on Earth was a reasonable one. War was not only a filthy business but it was an unintelligent one, and within the right framework of corporate organization, it could be repudiated. That framework had

27

come into existence and, because of it, rational human beings could put an end to war. The Treaty of Versailles was one part of that framework. The compulsory dismantling of the armed forces of a defeated enemy was to be accompanied in due time by the voluntary disarmament of the victors.

Alongside this negative programme, there was now a worldwide institution called the League of Nations, which was set up by the Allies shortly after the First World War in the lofty expectation that such an organization would by its nature prevent such a calamity happening again. I know that similar institutions had followed wars as far back as the Peloponnesian conflicts in Ancient Greece but, at long last, the lesson of their failure was being learnt and so the mistakes which had crippled previous Holy Alliances need not be repeated. The renunciation of war was now viable.

Anyone reading these words, and now equipped with hindsight, may wonder at the naivete of this optimism. What of the happenings in Russia? What of the 'Yellow Peril'? What of the national problems quite unresolved in Austro-Hungary and in the Balkans, to name but two areas of Europe which were festering with future disruptions. The answer lies in the profound change in general awareness of, and therefore attention to, political and social events in the world that has developed since those days.

At a superficial level the impact of radio and later of television has been revolutionary in that it has confronted everybody with information previously unavailable except to the powerful or the unusually diligent. The principle of 'out of sight, out of mind' operated to a degree that must seem incredible to the children of the wireless age, yet it played a large part in my pacifist confidence.

The recollection of the climate of opinion at a time when information was largely confined to notices on town hall walls and daily newspapers, is absolutely necessary for those who wish to understand the post-First World War days. The contrast comes alive for me as I remember walking down to Brockley Station from Aske's School at around four o'clock in the afternoon during the last days of the fighting in 1918, and hearing the newsboys calling out, '*Evening News*, *Star* and *Standard*', and watching people as they hurried from their front doors to find out what was happening.

Today we live in a radically different world. There are hourly news bulletins, an army of reporters, photographers and cameramen cover global events of greater and lesser importance. The impact of this availability of information cannot be overestimated. Indeed, of all the changes in the pattern of open-air meetings that I have held over the years, I would count the most significant as being within the audience itself. The average listener today is, superficially at least, much better informed about current issues and events than ever before.

It may be said that those who, like me, came to think of a future no longer haunted by the inevitability of war, were naive or possibly unwilling to face facts. Nevertheless, had we known more, had we gained access to many of those facts that were beyond our reach, then this rationalization of peacemaking would, I am afraid, have lost most of its certainty.

With that blessed capacity called hindsight, I am bound to reflect that the reasons for embracing pacifism which I have described were, for me, rationalizations rather than rational ones. I was, I can now see, infected by an emotional view of the horrors of war, a view which, as I have explained, presented a real danger to the morally-geared pacifism of my later years.

It may have been a reflection of the companionship I chose but it seemed to me at the time that this reaction to war was of profound significance to my contemporaries. There was this sense that we belonged to a generation which was on the move and which was fundamentally united. For me, the influence of Alex Wood, the Fellow of Christ's who was one of the leading Quakers and pacifists of the time, and Canon Woods, later to become Bishop of Lichfield, to say nothing of the impact of Beverley Nichol's anti-war polemic *Cry Havoc!*, probably contributed to a reaction against war and anticipation of peace that, all too soon, was to be revealed as being both superficial and premature.

Central to my growing commitment to pacifism was the development of religious faith, which I describe in a later chapter. At the time, I was taking a much keener interest in the basic requirements of the Christian faith, rather than the assumptions of that faith as had been represented in my Methodist upbringing. It is difficult to say now whether my increasing political awareness or religious involvement dominated my life and thoughts at Cambridge. On the one hand, it was the primary, if not the fundamental, nature of political events which prompted me to look more carefully at the assumptions of Christianity. On the other hand, my contact with religions and religious people in the university who were politically radical, had a profound effect.

If there was one man among my spiritual guides who confirmed my growing conviction that all I could hope to do or to be politically could be fully recognized and exploited in a religious vocation, it was the Methodist minister Henry Carter. A fervent peacemaker who was later to set up the Methodist Peace Fellowship during the 1950s, Carter was undervalued by his peers at the time and to a large extent unrecognized by his own Church as the prophet he was. Carter exercised an important influence on my life at that time and, many years later, I was privileged to say something of this at his memorial service. Henry Carter was one of my fathers in God.

While at Cambridge, I decided to offer myself as a candidate for the Methodist ministry. It would involve attending theological college and taking an apprenticeship in preaching, and was, of course, subject to my final acceptability. My pacifist convictions had prompted me to consider, for the only time in my life, whether I should offer my services to politics rather than to the Christian Church. Finally, I reached the decision that I have never regretted. Perhaps rather more easily than most people, I found myself able to look to a fulfilment that was both religious and political in my attempt to become a Methodist minister.

While I was reaching important decisions about my life, my commitment to pacifism did not take a particularly active form. Examinations were matters at which I had to work. So too were the routines of games and also my association with the Church. Now part of this indolence in the peace issue was little more than the working out of certain activities, but that was not a sufficient reason for remaining uninvolved with activities associated with peacemaking: I did so because I had no belief that such activities were necessary.

I was an unconscious victim of the mental and emotional process I have endeavoured to describe. From a combination of favourable auguries that were reasonable, and emotional processes which were not, I had come to assume that peace was assured. War would never again happen for two reasons: first, because man had come to his senses at long last and second, because the horror of war would somehow prevent its reappearance. We looked to the future with optimism. But how wrong we were was all too soon to be revealed.

CHAPTER THREE

MENTION THE FORUM on the Downs outside Dorchester and I suppose that most people will be reminded of a Roman occupation of parts of Britain long ago. For me it recalls with a vividness and immediacy which has nothing to do with ancient Rome, a public meeting there in 1936. It represents and brings to life a particular period associated with the issue of peace and war and a particular Anglican priest named Dick Sheppard whose personality coloured and typified for me the years leading up to the Second World War.

The meeting in question was a peace rally at which the principal speakers were George Lansbury with his famous bowler hat, his flat, ordinary voice and his blazing sincerity, Vera Brittain with all the prestige of her *Testament of Youth* and the fervour of a new-found faith, Laurence Housman, myself and, above all, the Reverend Dick Sheppard, leader of a campaign against war which had become for thousands a crusade for peace.

This rally had drawn the largest crowd I can remember for such an occasion and, in many respects, it was the high-water mark of the 'War We Say No' campaign which dominated my thinking in the early 1930s. By the middle of the previous decade the complacent, uninformed and uncriticized confidence in the prospects of peace had been washed away by a torrent of events, domestic and global, which compelled me and many others to realize how ill-founded was our confidence in a peaceful world, and how deceitful had been the emotional impulses which had buttressed that peaceful assurance. The kind of information which radio had started to provide, albeit slowly in the case of the significant and terrible events unfolding in Spain, produced an entirely different mood of scepticism rather than hope, of premonition rather than progress. Human affairs were not, after all, moving naturally and surely towards a better world, they were sliding irresistibly down the same paths which had led to previous disasters. Something, we believed, had to be done about it. It was this tide of opinion that led to the creation of the Peace Pledge Union and to the Dorchester peace rally, which was so largely identified with Dick Sheppard, Vicar of St Martin-in-the-Fields to 1927, Dean of Canterbury to 1931 and Canon of St Paul's till his death in 1937.

Sheppard was unquestionably the first 'radio parson' and his impatient preaching (he wrote a bestseller called *The Impatience of a Parson*) reached a nationwide audience both from the pulpit and over the air waves. My memories of Dick Sheppard are intimate and I still find it very moving to think about him. I remember quite clearly the first time we met and the immediate rapport we had which was to develop into the very close friendship that he was kind enough to offer me. He was a complex character, an aristocrat in the best sense of the word. He was afflicted with an asthmatic condition which repeatedly put him out of action. When he returned to his pulpit from such attacks he would describe in considerable detail how bad it had been and how well he was recovering.

Sheppard was a many-faceted character. He loved cricket and would organize and play games in the courtyard of St Martin-in-the-Fields. He was, believe it or not, an expert dancer and even won a competition in Paris. I remember seeing on the walls of his house many portraits of Napoleon Bonaparte, and I found to my great interest that he was apparently a descendant of Napoleon's.

I shall always be grateful to him for his magnificent sense of humour, which often more than compensated for what I think could be described as lack of theological depth in his preaching. He had charisma, coupled with a remarkable ability to win affection. For many, including myself, to meet him was the first step to discipleship. Although a very complex person in many ways, he allowed nothing to interfere with his uncomplicated peacemaking, and it was a mixture of that attractiveness and simplicity which, looking back, I found so irresistible. He was consumed almost physically by his passionate devotion to the cause of peace. In this he was a *dévot* rather than an advocate.

Increasingly, Sheppard's dominant theme became the threat of another war, the complacency of the Church to this approaching disaster, and what Christians in particular and people in general ought to do about it. 'War We Say No' became the slogan of his answer.

The story of 'War We Say No' and the 'Peace Army' which was its sequel, begins with a number of public utterances by Sheppard in which he invited those who felt as he did to join the ranks of what was to be an army of peace, and to put into practice the implications of saying 'No' to war. The first commitment of those who were prepared to join the Peace Pledge Union was a complete rejection of any participation in the war effort which, principally of course, involved a rejection of conscription. Looking back, I can see that those of us who were parsons were liable to agree rather too easily to something that we were not required in any case to do. Since we were not compelled to enlist, we were calling upon the laity to do something far more dangerous and difficult than anything we would have to face.

Sheppard's first recruit was Brigadier-General F. P. Crozier, a veteran commander from the battlefields of the Irish troubles. Dr Maude Royden, the greatest woman preacher I ever heard, joined soon after, as did Dr Herbert Gray, the author of *Men, Women and God*. I was the fourth recruit. Soon Laurence Housman, Lord Ponsonby, Gerald Heard, Aldous Huxley, A. A. Milne, Vera Brittain, George Lansbury, George Macleod and many others joined up in various degrees of parade-ground appearance to swell the ranks. It was, however, the great rallies inside and outside which seemed at the time to be the spearhead of advance for the 'Peace Army'. Of all these gatherings, I find the rally at Dorchester the most evocative of the essence of this whole episode in the quest for peace at that time. The meeting was later described by Vera Brittain in her book *Testament of Experience:*

My fellow speakers, I learned, were to be George Lansbury, the veteran Labour politician; the Rev. Donald Soper, already the best-known young orator in the Methodist Church, and Canon H. R. L. Sheppard, formerly Vicar of St Martin's. Our chairman was Laurence Housman, novelist and dramatist, who had just obtained permission from Edward VIII for his long-banned series of plays, *Victoria Regina*, to be shown on the London stage.

By the time my own turn came I was panic-stricken.

This Christian-pacifist platform was like no other on which I had stood; here my customary little speech in support of collective security would strike a discordant note. Its basis was political but the message of my fellow-speakers sprang from the love of God.

Yet I had prepared nothing else. Struggling to my feet I quoted Bunyan, improvised a feeble little story about the pilgrimage of the Anciens Combattants at Verdun, and sat down — the biggest disappointment to thousands on that spectacular afternoon.

The hilarious gaiety of the journey back to London all but obliterated this humiliation.

It was not long before the 'War We Say No' campaign entered a new phase. This came about by the moral revulsion of an ex-army padre to a repetition of the evils of warfare which he had known at first-hand. Dick Sheppard had been a chaplain in the First World War and felt an imperative moral command to refuse to go through it again. He must say 'No' to participation in any further conflict — and time was running out because such a conflict was appearing more likely every day. Those involved in the 'Peace Army' met to meditate with Huxley and Heard, to organize propaganda with Crozier, and to stand on platforms and declare their intentions at mass rallies.

From the very beginning Dick Sheppard, in particular, was convinced that the 'No' to war had to be married with a 'Yes' for peace. The concept of a peace army increasingly appealed to him and was shared by the rest of us. It is, however, one thing to vow that you will not willingly take part in war, to become a conscientious objector and take the consequences; but it is quite another actually to enlist in an alternative where no king's regulations or battlefield strategies exist.

All sorts of peaceful campaigns were canvassed. Let me describe one of them which like most, if not all of the others, began with the most practical of intentions only to founder, as Dick Sheppard said ruefully, on the 'rocks of impracticality'. Japan had invaded China and the Japanese army was at the gates of Chapei. The battle could be averted if an unarmed third army, an army of peace, were to take up its stance between the opposing forces. The intention was admirable, but the logistics of such an enterprise were simply impossible. How to get to China? There was talk of chartering a boat from Tilbury and, in fact, sundry members of the peace force went down to Tilbury ready and willing to set sail, but that was as far as the expeditionary force managed to get.

Meanwhile, the powerful elements in the international field were becoming more and more conspicuous and in a real though unfortunate way, the difficulties of peacemaking tended to undermine the credibility of the refusal to take part in warmaking.

After the Dorchester rally, recruitment to the 'Peace Army' dwindled. Dick Sheppard died and so, later, did Crozier. Sundry leaders of the campaign emigrated to the USA, while others like Lord Ponsonby, for whom I had very great respect, drew upon their political experience to remain convinced that there would be no war. Most of the rest of us, and I was small fry among them, drew what comfort we could from Chamberlain's umbrella and the somewhat pathetic hope that, even at the eleventh hour, man would 'forsake his foolish ways' and 'study war no more'.

As a community we did not say 'No' to war; no peace force stood between the combatants. When war broke out in 1939, I took small consolation in the thought that Dick Sheppard did not live to see his message and his hope disappear, temporarily at least, in four years of unparalleled violence and human tragedy.

I turn again to the reason for this attempted recovery of times lost or past. Just as the remembrance of my first reactions to war and peace as a child, and subsequent reactions as an undergraduate as epitomized in specific episodes, yield, if properly understood, important inferences which go far beyond their immediate context, so the experiences of the 1930s localized in the episode carry with them more general inferences for the continual question of war and peace.

The initial impact of the 'Peace Army' lay in the fact that Dick Sheppard appealed at the right time to a particular situation. The euphoria of the 1920s, always suspect, had been drowned in the economic depression, while Mussolini and later Hitler were personifying political programmes which the communist ideology had not anticipated, any more than the non-communist countries had realized the world-significance of the Marxist praxis. War could not be acceptable or glorious, nor could it be ignored as a past evil never to recur. It was on the way again and unless something very

35

practical was done, it would happen despite the horror with which men refused to countenance its reappearance.

Men and women must say 'No'. They could not change the social and economic forces which seemed to be combining to produce war conditions. Marxists might argue that the only way to produce such changes as would avert wars between the nation states, was by the insurgent power of a revolutionary proletariat, but that was a cure worse than the disease in that it baptized the very mass violence that peacemakers were concerned to avoid. There was a simpler, more direct path along which the peacemaker could travel: he, with like-minded ordinary people, could withdraw his labour. Dick Sheppard was calling for action, and to many like myself it offered the one alternative to the inertia of lying around waiting for international violence to happen and feeling powerless to prevent it. So we marched with banners and we attended our rallies and worked out the timetable of success.

I remember Aldous Huxley thinking aloud at a committee meeting in our headquarters overlooking Trafalgar Square, and concluding that the peace campaign could mobilize a million people who said 'No' to war and who would stick to that promise; no government could ignore such opposition and no war would therefore come about. It was stated at that meeting that our effective strength was something like three hundred thousand. We never reached the million mark. Moreover, the role of a peace army obviously depended on its size and its armaments. It was one thing to march around Piccadilly Circus with a placard advocating the way of conscientious objection to war, and I did this from time to time, but it was quite another to plan non-violent manoeuvres which would outmatch the processes of corporate violence. The truth is that we never found the equivalent in the war against war that the Salvation Army found in the war against the devil.

By 1939 the anti-war movement of the previous eight years or so had demonstrated that if nothing succeeds like success, nothing fails like failure. We had not been able to say 'No' to war. Our defeat was complete, except in the sense that, if the opportunity recurred, we could learn from our mistakes and half-truths.

I would offer two lessons that I learned from this experience. The first is the moral problem that lies within the simple appeal that Dick Sheppard, and of course many others, made to the individual to follow his conscience; to stand up and be counted. It is plainly true that, if enough people are prepared to oppose what officially their governments intend, then those governments can be halted in their tracks. But the establishment does not necessarily stand still while the forces against its activities are being mobilized.

The propaganda of the 'War We Say No' campaign was effective and commanded the abilities of extremely impressive public figures, but so was the propaganda on the other side effective. Again, the opposition to the whole concept of the 'Peace Army' was often not confined to words. I can remember some very lively meetings at Tower Hill and one or two quite dangerous ones. Dick Sheppard was asking for an attitude to peacemaking that went much further than advocacy. It was from his lips that I first heard the quip about the pig who complained to the hen that eggs and bacon for breakfast were all very well for the chicken who was only required to make a contribution, whereas for the pig it was a total commitment.

So the stronger the opposition and the nearer the peril of war, the clearer it became that the personal rejection of war in all its ways and works required a moral as well as an intellectual base.

As the conditions that prevailed in Hitler's Germany became clearer and as the evils of that regime became more obvious day by day, the pacifist position became more difficult to defend. More and more often, the question was posed as to whether a certain situation may not become so morally intolerable as to justify armed violence as the only method of dealing with it. Those of us who, as I have indicated, may have rather too easily declared ourselves opposed to war, made little attempt to answer this question. Was the moral argument against war sufficient to offset the practical demands of a given situation? I found that it was the substance of a Christian faith, however imperfectly understood, which still enabled me to maintain my initial commitment to say 'No' to war. A number of those who were with us in the Peace Pledge Union were not so committed and admitted that they found it increasingly difficult and finally impossible, in the light of the Hitlerite evil, to maintain that attitude of total renunciation of war.

As I have come now to understand and to believe, the moral argument is supreme. Armed violence against evil, however comprehensive and dastardly that evil may be, is not the way to overthrow it. The history book as well as the ethical argument confirms the pacifist case. It is finally impossible to cast out evil by evil, and the use of armed violence, however justifiable the cause, is a process of evil.

Years later, while sitting on a beach in Porth in Cornwall, I was to hear the news of the bombing of Hiroshima. The horror of it remains with me as I think about it. But by that time I had become very largely innoculated against the kind of emotions or reactions which no doubt I would have felt some years earlier. The same kind of dull ache rather than acute emotional pain came to me when I heard of the opening of the concentration camps. This compounding of horrors did not in any way affect my pacifism, although no doubt many would argue that it should have done. Hiroshima and Belsen, though matters of intense feeling, did nothing to disturb, but rather enhanced, the pacifist conviction.

That requirement of a faith as well as a programme was, back in those important years in the 1950s, all too frequently ignored. It was not enough just to oppose war intellectually for, when the tests came — and they began to accumulate before the outbreak of hostilities — many fell away. I am sure now that it was only because I believed that peace was already the divine purpose, as well as a human purpose, that I was able to stand firm. This is the first and dominant lesson from those pre-war experiences.

The second and almost equally valuable lesson has to do with our distinct failure to turn a protest into a proposition. The moment you ask more than one person to take action, you are committed to an organization and become involved in collective wishes. It may be a platitude but, looking back at the 'Peace Army', I can see its implication much more clearly than it appeared to the policy-makers in Dick Sheppard's camp.

Clausewitz's dictum that war is a continuation of politics is just as true of peace, whether or not Clausewitz thought so. It should be added that politics itself is the product of social and economic forces and possibilities. In other words, war is an element in a given society, it is part of a system, the output of institutions that are inseparable from the use of armed forces. To renounce war must therefore invoke the dismantling of the social and economic structure which not only encourages but also demands it.

By the same token peace is an element in a given society, part of a system, the output of institutions which depend upon the use of non-violent means. So a peace army can only operate as the agent of the sort of society which permits and requires its services. This

38

principle appears to be even more convincing as I reflect upon the subsequent movements towards peace which have developed since those early days of the Dick Sheppard movement.

Many times, it seems to me, the propositions set forth in international as well as national hopes for a more peaceful world have inevitably foundered on the rock of an insulated or individual programme which could only find the means of success within a much wider area of political and economic environment. The various international negotiations as between the Soviet Union and the United States, culminating in the SALT talks, seem to me to be a very powerful indictment of the proposition that peacemaking can be carried on independently of radical social and economic changes. We do not seem to have learned this lesson even yet, and it is in this particular regard that the conclusions to which I have come concerning this episode seem to me even more valid today.

The events I have described in this chapter convince me that peace is the fruit of justice and can grow on no other tree. It is impossible to graft it on to a society which is unjust. The rejection of war must go hand in hand with the rejection of the systems which have required war as a continuation of their politics. The perception of this truth did not make me a Marxist, as the outbreak of war in 1939 did quite a number of Dick Sheppard's disciples, but it did tie in with socialism with which I intend to deal later on in this book and which I now find is the other side of the pacifist coin.

CHAPTER FOUR

THE PROUSTIAN METHOD of the recall of times past by the remembrance of a particular event which characterizes and illustrates those times is, I find, less satisfactory in the recollection of wartime. I do not know whether my experience is shared, but the years of the Second World War and those which immediately succeeded them are a blurred memory, and I find the mood and mental climate of that period in my life difficult to recapture.

If war concentrates the mind, as in one obvious sense it does, it also narrows it. War is a prison as well as a slaughterhouse. Everything else is in abeyance except the process of armed conflict. Thinking about peace tends to become the occasional 'time off' from the consuming attention to the war effort. Nevertheless, there are two episodes in the period from 1939 to 1945 which do something to clarify those lost years and yield some overall considerations which are to me of value in the continuing quest for Peace on Earth and Goodwill Among Men.

During the blitz on London in 1940–1941, those who spent their nights at the underground stations would begin to surface between five and six in the morning when the sirens indicated that the bombers had gone home for the day. Many were hungry and those who had been sheltering in the Holborn tube found their way across the road to the West London Mission of which I was Superintendent Minister. There, every morning from 5.30 to 7.30, along with volunteers from the Mission, I improvised a canteen and a 'wash and brush up' service. The fare included eggs, bacon, toast and tea and the charges were minimal – I know, because I sat at the desk as cashier and those who could not pay seldom went away hungry. Our clientele included impresarios from Covent Garden, families from the tenements in Drury Lane, tired air raid wardens — all sorts of people collected in the strange bundle that war and perhaps little else can assemble.

What memories those days evoke! There was the man who removed his shoes to ease his feet, left the shoes under the table while he fetched his breakfast, only to find when he returned that someone else had put them on and departed in them; the difference between brown dirt and grey dirt — the former the more recently acquired, the latter the effect of days and weeks of neglect; the gratitude of so many in finding the warmth and comfort of such a canteen and, I must add, the surly complaints of others when the tea was not to their liking or we ran out of eggs.

That early morning canteen calls to mind many differing sorts of activities that went to make up the syllabus of my life as a pacifist minister responsible for a church during a time when I was not required to be a soldier, nor to be called up for national service. Yet, more important by far than any of these activities, was the recognition that, while 'War We Say No' is a practical proposition in times of peace, in wartime it is, in any absolute sense, impossible. As a conscientious objector, I could say 'No' to one form of service to the community in which I lived, but I could not escape my responsibility to make some other kind of contribution.

If, hitherto, I had thought of the role of the peacemaker to be to build a fence at the top of the cliff of war to prevent the wayfarer from falling over the edge, there was no way of arresting that fall; the best that could be done was to set up an ambulance service at the bottom of the cliff. Though it was possible for me to opt out of some activities in which my fellows were engaged, there was no earthly possibility, short of suicide, of opting out of the society in which I and they were bound together. So not only was I morally responsible for a positive role in conditions which precluded most of the programmes of peacemaking, I was at the same time involved in the corporate effort to fight and win a war whether I liked it or not.

In providing a rest centre for the bombed-out, as we in the Mission did, we were assisting the war effort by maintaining the morale of the citizen. In as much as I cooperated with the air raid wardens by roof-watching against fire bombs, I was an integral part of the defence mechanism. The problem was made more difficult for me because I was actually benefitting from those actions of my

41

fellow citizens which, as a pacifist, I both rejected and condemned. The food I ate was bought with the courage and blood of sailors in the Royal Navy and Merchant Service. I opposed the actions of those men, yet accepted the fruits of them. Such experiences raised a profound issue, which could be ignored in peacetime but was unavoidable under the conditions of war – in a word, 'compromise'.

Perhaps the most disturbing element in that compromise was a general unpreparedness to understand it and to deal with it. Personally, and as a member of the pacifist movement, I had to realize how unready we were either to relate it to basic ideas as beliefs, or to assimilate it within the pattern of non-violent behaviour. It was a brute fact which compelled one to realize how easy-going were the ideas which I had come to accept. When these ideas were confronted with the comprehensive end of mass killing they were, to some extent, inapplicable or, at best, only capable of partial expression. There was no action which could be isolated from the corporate life that was being lived and was, of course, endangered in a country committed to wholesale fighting.

It is this kind of experince which has brought home to me one of the most profound difficulties in carrying out the Christian faith – a difficulty which is unfortunately and regularly ignored by so much evangelical preaching. Once you know what is the will of God, by His Grace you can do it, for life is fundamentally a choice between what is manifestly evil and what is manifestly good. War is perhaps the supreme testing ground of such a simplistic faith and it seems to me incontestable that historically the Christian Church has avoided or watered down this supremely problematical issue.

I have often turned for comfort and reassurance to Pascal's *Provincial Letters*, which I regard as imperative reading for anyone concerned with the application of the Christian moral code. It is in this regard that the supremely scientific mind of Pascal reacts against the contorted argument of the Jesuits in order to accommodate the Christian faith to circumstances from which they are not prepared to depart. The problem is and must remain strictly insoluble but one in which humility and the need for forgiveness must play an equal part alongside the conviction of moral absolutes. Whatever their ultimate significance, they provided no comfortable bed in which I was able to lie during those war years.

For at this time, every individual action, short of death itself, was infected by the all-pervasive virus of war. As the doctrine of original

42

sin insists very properly, there is no completely pure intake of life-giving breath which is not somewhat contaminated in an atmosphere saturated with evil.

Meanwhile, the practical difficulties of peacemaking in wartime were considerable. Both my failures and successes are possibly worthwhile as a record of this question of compromise which, I believe, demands much more careful attention than it has even now come to receive.

In the absence of absolute guidelines, which are impossible to come by, the pacifist must choose more or less arbitrarily what he will do and what he will not do. There are areas in which he is free to act according to a clear conscience. He must find them and obey them. He can translate his conscientious objections to mass violence by refusing membership of the armed forces. He can opt out, whatever the cost, of direct participation in work which is equally clearly directed towards the prosecution of warfare. At the same time, he must choose to accept or to reject a whole range of ancillary services on the basis of a calculation as to whether such services belong essentially to the welfare of a society, whether it is at war or not, as to override the fact that they are at that specific time incorporated within the whole fabric of a nation at war.

Take, for example, the pastoral office of the Christian ministry. Was it necessary to offer the consolation of the Gospel to those whose public business it was to reject that same Gospel? I believed it was and conducted services, when asked, at RAF stations. I had to choose my words carefully and there undoubtedly was an element of compromise in that selection — I did not, for example, press the injunctions of the beatitudes. On balance, I have no regrets at trying to minister to men who were engaged upon activities which I regarded as being contrary to that Gospel.

I presumed to offer my advice to conscientious objectors who, like me, felt they dare not stand by idly while others were suffering the traumas of soldiering. To join the Royal Army Medical Corps was one option and many took it; to join the Friends' Ambulance Unit was, in my estimation, a better one, but there was no complete escaping from the net of national involvement. This was the melancholy lesson which I learned the hard way. I was to translate this experience in the 1950s, as I shall describe in a subsequent chapter.

I am sure it must appear strange and almost inexplicable to those who look back through other people's eyes at the general psychological environment in which these days were passed, but pacifists like myself were, in fact, allowed to argue in print and in the open air, and were not persecuted or threatened as possibly today it is assumed they would be.

There are two reasons as to why this was so. One is that, in my experience, a sincere presentation of one's difficulties alongside an equally sincere presentation of one's beliefs is recognized and respected. Secondly, the pacifist was not opting out of society — there were many ways in which one who was opposed to war could be profitably engaged in alleviating some of the miseries, difficulties and problems of war. I was fortunate enough to have a full-time job as a churchman and was responsible for all kinds of services which were manifestly for the good of the community, even in wartime. It was this kind of work that provided the wages of going on, even for a pacifist in wartime.

I am often told, however, that I enjoyed a certain privilege in as much as I was fairly well-known at the time and wore a dog-collar. It may well have been so and I have no doubt that other pacifists who were less lucky had a harder time of it.

Having been a budding broadcaster just before the war — I had both preached from St Martin-in-the-Fields and appeared regularly in a programme called *After Tea on Sunday* — I was now banned from the radio in wartime, and I have no complaint about that. Although the official line was hostile to my position, the actual behaviour of individuals was much more congenial.

Throughout the war, I spoke at Tower Hill and Speakers' Corner every week, except when we were occasionally compelled by air raids to seek cover. I well understood that I could not advance a pacifist procedure for a country committed to war, but nevertheless I could make a witness to a faith which, at that time, seemed inapplicable. To help to keep it alive for future use seemed imperative.

This outdoor exercise provided a wealth of revealing experiences of the time. I remember being warned by an anonymous police officer at noon one Sunday that there would be a round-up of speakers in Hyde Park that afternoon, so it would be judicious of me to carry my identity card. Then there was the man the authorities sent into the crowd who was to note down what I said and, I suppose, if necessary, use it against me in evidence afterwards. We struck up a very friendly relationship and I remember asking him on many occasions whether I was going too fast for him. He would nod or insist that I went over a particular passage again, which I was quite happy to do.

My message on these occasions may have been out of tune with the times, yet the crowd was invariably tolerant. I can only remember one or two occasions when I was knocked about a bit. To my shame, the tolerance was not always reciprocated. One Wednesday at Tower Hill I was questioned by a member of the crowd who objected strongly to what I was saying. He was not a very good speaker and the longer he persisted the more incoherent he became and the more I was able to serve off him, perhaps making him look somewhat ridiculous. I enjoyed the experience, I'm afraid, until he suddenly abandoned his stridency and said, 'I wonder how you would feel if your brother had been killed in the desert as mine was last week.' I can feel to this day my own reaction and that of the crowd. We had been taken by the scruff of our human necks out of the realm of argument and into a realm where reason cannot suffice and argument becomes impertinent. I should have understood this from my student days when I learned from the works of Lotze that reality is richer than thought. It took the war to bring home that truth, and that occasion on Tower Hill to bring it to focus and to recognize its effects.

Pacifism is not a creed independent of all other elements except the element of rationality. Its moral demands do not simply follow from sources which relate to a human being as 'homo sapiens'. What a man thinks depends in so large a degree on what he feels. There surely can be no such thing as a course of action promoted entirely in the cold light of reason. I was to discover that, in the presentation of the pacifist case, you can win your case and lose your man. Arguments are only persuasive when they are not in collision with strong emotions – and nothing creates emotions so dominating as does war.

So unless the appeal to peace pays as much attention to this emotional background as it does to the intellectual foreground, it will fail to convince. This is partly what is meant by the assertion that hitherto the advocates of peace have not succeeded in finding a moral equivalent for war.

Peace as a passion is as necessary as peace as a programme. The bereaved man on Tower Hill taught me that the way of non-violence must be supported by the power that the fellowship of suffering can interfuse with the fellowship of reason. Its emotive capacity has not as yet been sufficient to counteract the emotive ingredients in a war mentality and condition.

A further lesson that I learnt during these war years was that life is by no means as tidy as thought. We may be able to make up our minds so that there appears to be nothing left over, but when it comes to making up our lives there is no such experience that enjoys the quality of neatness. Our feelings never completely tally with our convictions and we have to settle for an approximate relationship between the two. For example, I found it impossible to be as single-hearted in my pacifism as I was able to be single-minded. I listened avidly to the news with an increasing desire that the Allies should win, alongside the conviction that the campaign for military victory could not in the end win peace or justice. Looking back, I remember the satisfaction with which I heard of Montgomery's exploits or Russian victories and, worse, still entertained a sneaking regard for the whole bloodthirsty practice of the martial arts.

I have reproached myself many times since for this inconsistency. Indeed, I remember a considerable uneasiness at the time that I seemed to be two people and therefore something of a hypocrite. With no attempt at a whitewash, I would venture to say that then and now, a complete integrity between one's thoughts and one's emotions is out of reach.

If, with the best of intentions, a perfect correlation between the world of thought and that of feeling is practically unattainable, such a situation does not necessarily call for penitence and the determination to amend. What it does is to emphasize a working rule. Emotions can be the servants of principles reached by enlightened reason, but they cannot without disaster become their master. Where thoughts and feelings do not coincide, as happens in wartime for those who are would-be peacemakers, one must stick to the deliverance of rational judgment, trying not to be too concerned that one belongs to a world which, in many other ways, is 'booming, buzzing confusion'.

Whenever I am inclined to take too easily the Christian doctrine of free will and especially the corollary that, whatever the outward circumstances, man can preserve his spiritual identity, I remember what in many respects was the most traumatic experience I have ever lived through. Some years after the war, I went to Auschwitz. I was paying an official visit to the Methodists in Poland – there were not

46

many of them, and they were all heroes. My guide was a pastor who had survived Auschwitz and knew his way about the dreadful place.

The Russians had frozen the prison camp after liberating the survivors. The whips were still lying on the cell floors, petrol syringes were still lying on the tables in the extermination area, the rags of clothing were everywhere, the ovens seemed barely cool, and the door to the deadly, so-called 'bathroom' was covered, every inch of it, with graffiti – the last messages of those about to be gassed.

To compound this horror, my guide showed me the gruesome evidence of the tidy-mindedness of the German authorities – a barn full of hair, a room full of children's toys, another piled high with surgical appliances and the wooden legs of seemingly countless victims of this juggernaut of evil. The marvel to me was that anyone could maintain the marks of human dignity in such a terrible environment.

For comfortable parsons to prate about 'the royalty of inward happiness and the serenity which comes from living close to God' is nauseating impudence. All the more so for a yet more terrifying condition which the inmates of Auschwitz underwent before death released them from their tortures. The walls of one of the main corridors were lined with the photographs of the prisoners, all of whom looked alike, and no wonder – shave the prisoner's head, remove glasses or teeth, put him or her into the regulation indistinguishable smock, feed the prisoner on a diet calculated to kill in three months, and what is left of human identity?

Auschwitz, as nothing else in my experience except intolerable pain, has remained a constant reminder of the extent to which a human being can be so depersonalized as to appear to make qualities such as dignity, forbearance and individuality nothing more than words from a dead language.

Yet this is not the whole story and, for the more hopeful part of it, I remember with profound gratitude the Polish guide who took me to the camp. He saw me off to the airport and as I was about to leave, hesitatingly asked whether I could do him a small service when I got home. He said that somebody had told him of a particular lotion, unavailable in Poland, which counteracted a hair condition and prevented it from falling out. Would I be so kind as to send him some of this healing lotion? Of course, I readily agreed, and almost casually asked him if he could remember any circumstances which might have contributed to this balding process.

47

He answered: 'I think it probably started when I was in Auschwitz. You see, every Sunday morning ten of my block were taken into the execution yard. One of us was shot and the other nine were returned to the block. I think it had something to do with the tension of standing there and wondering whether this week you were the one to be shot.'

What a man! I sent him the hair lotion, though I never heard whether or not he ever received it. He is dead now but his spirit lives – a spirit of indomitable courage and, above all, a spirit free from bitterness, a testimony to the unconquerable power that enables lesser mortals, like me, to hold fast to the Christian faith, to hope and to love, even as I think of Auschwitz.

Looking back on the war years, I do not repine overmuch that my feelings wandered from the straight and narrow path which, as Pascal's 'thinking reed', I had thereto followed. On the other hand, I am grateful for the experience because it provided an assurance that the quest for Peace on Earth need not wait upon a watertight and impeccable case that is as convincing to the mind as it is to the heart. What happened in the years following the end of the Second World War provides a realistic comment on this claim.

*With my younger brother and sister, Sos and Millicent,
in 1917*

Captain of the Cricket XI at Aske's School, Hatcham

(Keith Ellis)

Addressing the crowd at Tower Hill in the twenties

Tower Hill in the forties

With the delegation of British churchmen who visited Russia to persuade the Orthodox Church to attend the Evanston Conference in 1954 of the World Council of Churches. The Patriarch is seated in the centre and I am on his right

Leading the CND protest march from London to Aldermaston on 5 April 1958

CHAPTER FIVE

IT RAINED ALL day. The occasion was the Saturday of the first CND march to Aldermaston in 1958. Canon John Collins, the first leader of the Campaign for Nuclear Disarmament, had deputed me to lead the marchers and by nightfall we were halfway there. As I recall that particular day, it brings back to me the aura even more than the events of CND in the 1950s. There was something in it of a crusade, for it captured much more than political and even moral loyalties in its quest for peace. I still find it illuminated by the glow of inspiration and a vision that went far beyond its practical and immediate aims.

Let me give two personal recollections, which are not only true but precious as I live through them again. As a person committed to church services on Good Friday and Easter Day, it had been for years a family understanding that we would spend the Easter Saturday together on some kind of outing. I had delayed telling my wife that I was going to break this family tradition to go marching instead. When finally I broke the news and asked for her understanding, she replied to my astonishment that it was perfectly all right. She had hesitated to tell me, but she had also arranged to join the march with our eldest daughter and some friends. This air of spontaneity was further emphasized when, as we halted in the Methodist Hall at Slough to be warmed by tea (though not dried out), another of our daughters was among the volunteer waitresses. We had had no idea that she, too, was with the march.

CND was an eucumenical pilgrimage that numbered all sorts of people, drawn together first and above all by what must surely be recognized as a spiritual impulse, and one which was self-validating

– 'Here I stand, or here I march, I can do no other'. This is not an extravagant claim to be made on their behalf. I am persuaded that, for a great many such pilgrims to Aldermaston, CND was becoming a way of life and that, after all, is what religion is. Whatever was to happen to CND in its later manifestations, I can still recapture the spirit of those early adventures to and from Aldermaston: the speeches and crowds at Trafalgar Square, the inner satisfaction, the sense of vocation enhancing the sense of conviction. Yes, I reflect that it was a crusade for the sake of Peace on Earth.

Of its decline during the sixties and seventies I shall write later, but here I will relate the second personal recollection which typifies another of the more fundamental characteristics of CND. We were slushing along past Heathrow when I noticed a group of men and women standing by the roadside in the drenching rain. As we passed, the men took off their hats to us and stood bareheaded. I can imagine the cynic suggesting that they were showing respect, as was the custom in my youth, in the presence of a funeral hearse. Nothing of the sort. They were members of the local municipal council and, as I found out afterwards, had been standing there for hours waiting for us. They were indeed showing respect for the cause which the march represented, but of course they could have done that with their hats on. As one of them told me years afterwards, their hats came off almost instinctively and although he could not have put his motive for so doing into precise words, respect was not enough – for that which those councillors recognized in the march was something which invited reverence.

I know the impression it made upon me, a mixture of pride and humility, a catch in the throat and a not, I trust, unworthy sense that, if there were a holiness about peace that there could not be about war, then those councillors recognized it and proclaimed it.

At the same time, this second reminiscence sheds a clear light on another characteristic aspect of CND which distinguished it from the former activities of the 'War We Say No' movement. The dropping of the atomic bomb and the prosecution of nuclear methods of warfare had dramatically changed the entire scenario since the days of that Boer War sentry. The use of atomic and later nuclear energy in the evolutionary process of firepower had disturbed the measured increase in the lethal capacity of weapons which had prevailed for centuries. Gunpowder had previously transformed the situation in which the crossbow was superior to the bow and arrow, but in degree rather than in kind. For hundreds of years even, the use of gunpowder was only marginally more efficient. The firepower of Nelson's battleships at Trafalgar, for example, was not more than eight per cent more lethal than that of Drake's ships against the Armada.

But the discovery and use of the atomic bomb created a situation in human affairs similar to that which apparently happens in the evolutionary process itself – a hitherto unknown mutation in which that process is irreversibly transformed. Whatever the argument, the fact is inescapable. From 1945, the issue of war and peace would never again be as it was before Hiroshima. This new unprecedented situation goes far to explain the emergence of the CND and, in particular, its differences from the traditional campaigns against mass violence.

This would seem to me to be an example of the way in which horror and fear need not be totally rejected as quite false instruments to be used in the quest for peace. As a spur to action they may have their place, in that they may jerk people out of a complacency or an attitude of indifference. The problem, of course, is not to utilize this fear and horror as a means to the end, but merely as the gate into the field of other kinds of activity.

For example, the centre of attraction moved away from the individual and the attitude he took to such questions as conscientious objection to soldiering, and in its place came the attention to the instruments of that mass violence and the corporate repudiation of those instruments by the State. To get rid of the 'war wish' was still the philosophy of peacemaking, but now the politics of peacemaking was disarmament. With the zeal and devotion which animated those committed to ending evil were now added two powerful riders.

First were the appalling prospects that threatened everybody in a nuclear age, and were the more ominous because of the Cold War in Europe and the very real wars in Korea and later in Vietnam. While a fearful desire to 'flee from the wrath to come' as I have previously argued can be as craven as it is counterproductive, nonetheless this new situation of cosmic peril could be used to awaken citizens to the need to do something in the light of the new threat which faced them.

The companion rider to this fear was the concept of reducing the threat of mass nuclear violence by corporate action. This seemed to many a man and woman in the street to be practical politics, not necessarily dependent on a personal pacifism nor even a unanimous public opinion. Further, it seemed a welcome relief from the nagging suspicion that the quest for peace was hopeless, man being what he is. Government by public action could and must do what individuals, however united in voluntary association, will always fail to achieve.

Here was the deeper meaning behind the attitude of those local councillors as I remembered it. Dick Sheppard's aim, which we had shared, was so to mobilize an army of peace as to confront the government of the day, thereby forcing it to change its policy. The aim of those councillors was, consciously or unconsciously, to utilize the forces of government to enable people to change their minds and to mend their ways. So the paradox within CND was that it found its acceptability both among those who appreciated and responded to the spiritual call to a crusade and among those who, conscious of the new perils of war, joined themselves to a campaign which was all the more practical because it made fewer demands on the individual and was primarily the responsibility of the civil authority.

I would not for a moment imply that such less than noble motives belonged to that group which greeted us at Heathrow, but I am satisfied that they were symptomatic of both the strength and the subsequent failure of CND to achieve its goal. Of the more general reason for that failure (at least before its resurrection in the eighties), I shall treat in the concluding chapter of this first part of the book, because that reason is not confined to CND but applies, as I believe, to every movement against war except the absolute pacifist one.

Although the CND of the fifties temporarily captured the Labour Party, and although it enlisted a formidable group of responsible men and women to fight its more difficult battles, it never succeeded in setting nuclear disarmament in the kind of economic and political environment which alone could keep it viable. The evidence for this criticism can be found in the breakaway Committee of One Hundred, and in the story of Bertrand Russell's adventures in trying to set up an international peace forum, which organization still exists though with inconsiderable effectiveness.

It is the underlying assumption, however, which demands examination. Granted that the political implications of disarmament were recognized in CND literature, and by no means ignored by such politicians as Michael Foot and others who took part in the great Trafalgar Square rallies, the true relationship between disarmament and the political and economic conditions within which it was being advocated were never pressed, as they should have been. I was as guilty in this regard as others involved in the movement.

Although it would be unfair to say that nuclear disarmament was being proclaimed in a vacuum and isolated from other elements in society, the effort was repeatedly made to urge its claims as if the fulfilment of them were an option capable of being undertaken independently of corresponding changes in the society as a whole. I have already insisted that someone who says 'no' to war does not, by that affirmation, however sincere, enjoy the liberty of complete adherence to such a repudiation. In so much as the air he breathes is contaminated by war, much that he believes and propounds will be invalidated until his lungs can inhale an air free of that infection.

So the postponement of disarmament is similarly inhibited because he must draw his breath from an environment that can stifle rather than invigorate him. This stark fact was brought home to me when in discussion around that time with peaceworkers in California. They assured me that more than fifty per cent of all the industries in that part of America were either directly or closely associated with the armaments business. Disarmament would, in consequence, create a situation of chaos if it were undertaken independently of radical changes in the general complexion of social life. Further, those changes could not be regarded as consequences of a disarmament programme which would inevitably take place in an orderly and rational fashion. Indeed, the dismantling of the war machine would be ruled out of hand by those dependent for their livelihood on jobs within armaments industries, and their maintenance. Or, if it were pushed through in the way, years ago, that the Volstead Act against the drinking of alcohol pushed through a prohibition programme for the whole of America, it would have no chance of long-term survival. Even while it was on the statute book, it would bring not only the law but the whole issue of disarmament into contempt.

I found that what those Californians said was entirely convincing. In fact, their argument was applicable in any society where the economy is saturated with or is considerably involved in the making and selling of arms. In other words, mass violence is an integral

53

element in a modern society. The economy depends upon its prosecution and the nation state itself is based on the ultimate sanction that its armed forces are deemed to provide.

The CND to which I was devoted flourished because it appealed to impulses deep enough to find a responsive echo in the hearts and minds of all sorts of people. It started as a crusade but, like its famous predecessors, it foundered into temporary failure because it did not marry its intention to get rid of weapons with an equal intention to get rid of the system which required them.

It was at about this time that I used to meet Michael Foot quite regularly and, not unnaturally on these occasions, we would discuss theology as well as politics. Michael was very largely responsible for the success of *Tribune*, which at that time seemed to be, along with the *New Statesman*, the standard-bearer of true socialism. I felt that *Tribune*'s effectiveness would be enhanced if it presented a spiritual dimension comparable with its political one, and Michael's response was to invite me to write some articles. The correspondence that these pieces provoked – both for and against – over the following twenty years, during which time I was a regular contributor, were in my view a justification for the widening of the *Tribune* case and convinced me of the indissoluble link between overall political aims and the necessity of disarmament if its objectives were to be successful.

The vicissitudes of the CND campaigns established this truth for me, and now I was compelled to face its sequel: what system would be congenial to the aims and enterprise of disarmament as the prevailing system was not? Although such a question is sufficiently daunting, even now, to try to bypass it and to concentrate on what appears to be the simpler and more rewarding effort of reducing the more terrible of the weapons, there is no escape, as I see it, from the need to go on a crusade for a different social order with the same urgency with which so many went and joined CND. I should add that I have made up my mind long since, and that I do know what the new system required to usher in and to nourish disarmament must be.

It must be a socialist system.

CHAPTER SIX

HAVING BEEN BROUGHT up in a deeply religious way, I was aware from an early age of the doctrine – indeed the expectation – of the end of the world. This apocalyptic element in the Christian prognosis was but vaguely noticed until I was exposed to its significance at a Mission meeting at which I was invited to consider the spiritual peril which threatened me, unless I made my peace with God immediately. The urgency was there because God in His inscrutable wisdom was about to bring His creation to a sudden end – the exact date may be unannounced, but there was no time to be lost.

I noticed after a time that it did not happen and was neither permanently bothered emotionally by this terminal prospect, nor later impressed with its credibility. But I shall never forget the fright it gave me at the time and the entirely different effect it had upon me, compared with every other attitude or reaction that went to make up my conscious life. The fact that it is a religious concept which today is incredible to the thinking person and which contains an element of immorality completely inconsistent with the eternal love of God, does not alter the traumatic effect it had on me as a young man. Only those exposed to such an experience and against a background which tended to create a disposition to be convinced by such evangelical pressures, can, I suggest, appreciate how powerful can be the impact of such apocalyptic warnings. To think of the Streatham Methodist church where it happened to me all those years ago is still to taste the salt in my mouth, though the idea has long since left my head.

It is this unique recollection from my early life which came to me during the fifties and sixties when I found the concept of a divine apocalypse transferred to a human setting. I had the same emotional reaction to the future in respect of peace and war that, years before, I had felt about the end of the world.

In fact, the end product of both these final events was the same. The difference was that, whereas the divine apocalypse had been set specifically within God's power, and there was nothing we could do about it except to prepare ourselves for its inevitable actuality, this new, fearsome end of the world we had now taken out of God's hands. Hitherto man's destructive power had been limited, though, as I have described earlier, it had increased with appalling rapidity. Now the development of nuclear power had ushered in an era of quite unprecedented effects.

Until this time, however devastating the effects of war might be, it was at least possible for the survivors of such a disaster to pick up enough of the pieces to make a living. The shock of having to contemplate obliteration of everything moral rather than the prospect of some continuing possibility of 'life after death', was an overwhelming condition in which thought and feeling took on a new intensity. I tried to express myself in those terms in the open air and I found it difficult to understand the comparative complacency with which most of the crowd received my apocalyptic warnings. Maybe the emotional elements in what I was saying were too much a hangover from my experience of a metaphysical 'judgment day'. Maybe I was perfervid rather than fervent. Maybe I put it rather unconvincingly. In any case, the fact remains that, in the years 1955–1970 and indeed beyond, the implications of what the arms programmes were heralding did not receive the kind of awesome attention which they demand. So let me attempt some reflection on this global and final situation which emerges from those years.

First and overriding all other considerations, war can no longer be conceived and practised as a means. It is an end in itself. In the days of the Cold War, the Berlin Blockade, the Cuban missiles crisis and Korea, war was still considered as being capable of producing certain effects. It could be lost, as happened to the USA in Vietnam. It could be won, or at least could achieve certain objectives, as in Korea. There were always practical options and the risks taken could be justified by the possibility, however remote, of the attainment of positive results. Wars could achieve things. It was obviously desirable to avoid the trauma that would inevitably accompany even a victorious war, but it was not the worst of evils. There were some things that could conceivably be worse than war. It might be the darkest of tunnels through which a nation had to travel but, however long as well as dark that tunnel, there was a light at the end of it. That was the argument.

With the development and proliferation of nuclear weapons, which took place in this period immediately following the 'bell-wether' function of the atomic bomb, that light — if indeed it was ever more than an hallucination — had been extinguished. There now remained only one option — to prevent war breaking out. For, once it had, everything was irretrievably lost.

There is, of course, a counter-argument which still appears to offer comfort to those convinced that this apocalyptic approach to war in the nuclear age is an assumption rather than a certainty. It is the strange contention that the possession of the nuclear weapon, with its horrifying effects, is an assurance that it will not be used. Moreover, mutuality in the possession of the weapon by contending forces will double-lock that safety door.

Logistically this idea is surely absurd. Escalation of weapons is the essence of successful warfare. Furthermore, the argument assumes that wars are conducted by logicians, whereas it is all too evident that the power unleashed in battlefields corrupts those who use it so that, whatever the ultimate consequences of using particular weapons and foregoing the use of others, the immediate advantage will totally mask any more ultimate effects. Those whom the gods destroy and those whom the gods watch destroying each other, they first make mad. War is mass lunacy, whatever the initial rationality of those who practise it.

No weapon will be excluded if, in the delirium of conflict, it produces the appearance of success. And, indeed, what is this conventional war from which the optimists believe nuclear weapons will be excluded?

What of chemical warfare and biological warfare and what of the products of research into even more terrible instruments of mass suicide? No one tells the truth about the armaments which will be deployed in any future conflict. Winston Churchill said, 'Lying in wartimes is an indispensable ally', and I have no doubt that he would have expected that ally to be equally loquacious in the preparation for a war, or indeed the build-up of resources against its occurrence.

A further claim rests on the fact that, for more than thirty-eight years, peace, or something approaching it, has existed between the two superpowers. This time-lag between wars is presented as if it contains a philosophical as well as a temporal truth. It is still, as I write, the corner-stone of the argument for the maintenance of the nuclear capability. I submit that it is no such thing. The interval between wars is determined by many factors and not one of them can reasonably aspire to any kind of philosophical certitude. The human story hitherto is clear. A war occurs as a result of two conditions which coincide: the one is the tinder, and the readiness of the means to undertake it; the other is the wild, unpredictable spark which ignites that tinder – Jenkins' ear, the Ems telegram, Sarajevo, Danzig are among the motley collection of such sparks. They belong to the category of *casus belli*, but the *casus belli* is the war readiness that is a characteristic of the nation state. I shall develop this theme in the second part of this book which will be concerned with the politics of the Christian Gospel, since I am here concentrating on the peace which Christianity promises. Suffice it to say at this point that having escaped until now from the outbreak of a Third World War is a coincidence, worthless as an argument, and diversionary in as much as it distracts attention from the grim fact that, so long as the tinder is there, there will be sparks to ignite it.

These awesome considerations have, I am sure, fundamentally affected human attitudes within our society. I would use the mood of the crowds in Hyde Park as evidence that, in the period I am attempting to describe, and even more so in the 1970–1980 period, there has been a degree of cynicism about nearly everything that I do not recollect from even the thirties. I am satisfied that this is the product of an increasing sense of hopelessness in the international situation and particularly in the arms race which seems to be an essential part of it.

In this connection I am greatly disturbed at the apathy of so much organized religion, and apathy for a believer is indistinguishable from cynicism. I see, on the other hand, the re-emergence of CND now as a wholesome reaction to that cynicism. The demand for action seems all the more imperative in a situation which has become even more ominous, if that were possible, than that of the fifties. So the recruiting has begun afresh, and now CND can see itself as a movement alongside peace movements in Western Europe and across the Atlantic. Better still, it appeals to those who, like myself, find a deeper emotion of urgency because of the terminal elements that the nuclear development has inserted into the entire issue of peace and war.

For some, the relative lack of impact of peacemaking at this time has produced a withdrawal into carelessness and cynicism. For others, it has intensified this concern. But how to express that concern? Demonstrations at the gates of war factories, marches to Aldermaston, squatting in Trafalgar Square are not enough. What 'direct action' can disarmers take to awaken the indifferent, give hope to the impotent and change the policies to which they are opposed?

In the thirties, there had seemed to be two simple equations. One hundred thousand citizens saying 'No' to war and ready to pay the price of that refusal equals failure. One million citizens making the same decision and ready to stick by it equals success. The first equation was obviously accurate, and the second never got further than an hypothesis.

Two decades afterwards, when CND shifted the emphasis away from the individual and towards corporate political action, the equations were more or less the same. To capture a major political party and to obtain its commitment to nuclear disarmament equals success. To infiltrate a major political party or parties with CND supporters without securing that party's commitment equals failure. CND did, in fact, capture the Labour Party, but only to demonstrate that the second of these equations was, as it turned out, fallacious.

The defection by Aneurin Bevan with his famous objection to entering the council chambers of the world naked as Foreign Secretary, and the fact that the Labour Party did not enter an election under the CND colours, left the equation as hypothetical as was the earlier one. I sensed at the time, and that impression is reinforced as I reconsider the time of the early CND, that political emphasis on disarmament and peacemaking tends to obscure the moral dynamic of a personal vocation.

While the vicissitudes of my eighty-one years have served to strengthen my commitment to non-violence and the pacifist cause, there is behind this quite fundamental belief, which may be regarded as the strategy of peace, the question of the precise tactics of peacemaking. To counter the accusations so often levied at members of the cloth that we are long on general truths but decidedly short on their particular application, I will try to illustrate the practical moral problems of the peacemaker by comparing the CND campaign of the fifties and sixties with that of today.

First, the common denominators; CND has never veered from its commitment to disarmament in the nuclear field. Both campaigns were led by clerics, Canon John Collins in one and Monsignor Bruce Kent in the other. Both campaigns have commanded the support of specialists in the nuclear field, or at least in its ramifications, like Ritchie Calder in the first and E. P. Thompson now. Both have attracted the enthusiasm and support of significant figures in every walk of public life. In these respects the similarity is clear: CND in its first and second incarnation has presented the moral, intellectual, and practical case for disarmament. Beginning in the nuclear field is the genuine hope for general disarmament and peace on earth. But it must be admitted that CND in the first campaign did not succeed and that in the second it is still a minority movement.

To understand why this should be so can, I believe, be seen in an examination of the differences between the two campaigns. First of all, there was a difference of mood, if 'mood' is not too superficial a word. In the fifties we marched and countermarched on a crusade which could be explained, as we thought, with the simplicity and infallibility of a modern Peter the Hermit, and although Canon Collins, for whom I had the greatest of respect, was never able to electrify that crusading spirit in his leadership, there was time to reach Jerusalem and the road was open. Furthermore, the developments within the Labour Party and the support of world figures like Bertrand Russell, seemed to augur victory.

The mood of the contemporary CND is markedly different. Not surprisingly, the apocryphal element is much more pronounced and the time factor is more urgent. Secondly, whereas in the earlier campaign the question of deterrence played a minor role, the recent outburst of CND activity has been opposed by a counterproposal.

During the fifties there was little point in claiming that the underlying intention of CND to prevent another war from breaking out was entirely dependent upon accepting the programme of totally abandoning the nuclear arsenal. The world was still recovering from the trauma of a war. Keeping the peace lay in the future; there had not been sufficient time-lag in the fifties and sixties from which to argue.

The argument now of the government in the eighties is derived from hindsight. It is claimed that the peace has been kept. The horrific dangers of a Third World War have not happened. Something other than disarmament has kept the peace. The reciprocal capacity of the two great powers to incinerate each other and to begin to do it in four minutes has produced a balance of terror.

So goes the argument against the second CND, and it introduces a case for war avoidance which would have been impossible to propound at a time when the great powers were still licking their wounds. Moreover, the principle of mutual deterrence which was practically successful, so the argument goes, could even be blended with peacemaking by a continuous pressure for multilateral disarmament which would both maintain a balance of power but progressively lessen its overall awesome capacity.

The first and second CND campaigns have been resolutely unilateralist but the difference has been that, whereas in the fifties and sixties, nuclear disarmament for many of its supporters was a *cri de coeur* for the survival of a future generation, it had to argue within the framework of a defence system which claimed the warrant of history, and demanded NATO as indispensable within the framework.

Only very recently has CND come to recognize that a policy of unilateral nuclear disarmament on the part of one member of NATO (which already has the nuclear arms of its senior partner based on its own shores) must involve the abandonment of NATO itself by that member state. It is all the more significant because of recent statements made by Neil Kinnock that, if the Labour Party were re-elected, they would indeed get rid of all nuclear weapons. This surely raises in a critical and final manner the question as to whether it is possible to remain in a NATO alliance while objecting to and refusing to take part in one of its main programmes. I, for one, am quite convinced that it is totally impossible so to do.

I have found it surprising that CND did not see earlier than its 1983 conference that nuclear deterrence and membership of a nuclear alliance is a contradiction in terms. To me, the argument against multilateralism is clear. Multilateralism is not a primary stage, it is a secondary one and assumes but does not define the action of which it is the product. Unilateralism is a first step and all respectable ethics would agree that there is no substitute for such an initiative. Multilateralism is a vehicle without a self-starter. It is

61

relevant to the present discussion to underline the results of the attempt so far to foster peace by the method of collective security under the multilateral umbrella. The situation is getting worse not better. There exists between the superpowers a situation of 'cold war'. The attempt to achieve parity is a nonsense. Plans for mutual oversight of nuclear armouries have invariably run into the ground, and the SS20s, 21s and 22s on the one side and the Pershing and cruise missiles on the other, have not succeeded in restoring a balance of terror, but instead have caused the breakdown of recent international conferences that might have made some progress.

It is here that I find the pacifist case at its strongest. The deterrent argument enshrines a principle which is only worthy of a decent burial and crystallizes the moral conditions upon which the entire process depends. Multilateralism is based on the proposition that east is east and west is west and never the twain shall meet except in some sort of battlefield. Deterrence presupposes a malignant relationship on both sides; what is more, that mutual assumption of the other's evil intent is susceptible of only one treatment and that is to frighten the evil opponent with disaster if he proceeds with his villainy.

You are either a cowboy or an Indian. You are a proletarian pacifist or a capitalist thug. This is the moral monstrosity lurking within the multilateral assumption. Past failure in resolving the issues at stake only serves to strengthen your quite impudent confidence that the other side is incorrigibly wicked and that your side is right. For me to accept this as a moral basis upon which to build a world of peace would invalidate everything I have learned as to the possibility of goodness overcoming evil. It is the depth of cynicism, for it paralyzes at its source those more kindly aspirations for goodwill in which many international conferences begin, but which invariably wither in the hothouse of mutual accusation and suspicion.

Only unilateralism can introduce in the place of this intellectually and morally unworthy position a creative moral optimism which invests a conference with hope and unfreezes the prolonged rigidities of a world which is conceived as containing only two sides – the goodies and the baddies.

Unilateral action must be total and unconditional in the sphere of mass violence. Nothing less than the unilateral non-violent approach to the erstwhile enemy today will be heart-warming

62

enough to unfreeze the 'cold war' in this year of Our Lord 1984.

But perhaps the most startling difference between the two CND campaigns is the emergence in the second of what could be called the Greenham Common factor. Aldermaston and Greenham Common are not the same. The demonstrators of Greenham Common are not just the successors to the Aldermaston marches and 'sit-ins'. These women, and some of them worshipped at Kingsway Hall, have brought into CND a new spirit of valour and personal sacrifice. They have identified a particular development of NATO policy, which is to deploy some of its theatre nuclear arsenal in Europe and particularly those weapons which are mobile and therefore cannot be destroyed in their static bunkers. They can be fired from almost anybody's back garden almost anywhere in these islands.

But there is another aspect of the contemporary CND and Greenham Common campaigns which raises the whole issue of violence in a more acute form than hitherto. It is the degree of physical force that can properly be enlisted in the cause of disarmament. There is a perceptible difference, for example, between sitting down at the gates of Aldermaston, as with many others I did, and pulling down fences on the perimeter of the Greenham Common base, as some of these determined women are trying to do. Again, there is a perceptible difference between sitting down in Trafalgar Square and preventing no one (except the pigeons) from going about their lawful occasions, and blocking the highway leading to a nuclear base, attracting a physical response from those entitled to use that highway, and not only those seeking access to the said base. Although it would be inaccurate to draw too precise a distinction between the two types of official CND protest, the fact remains that a degree of physical violence is involved in the tearing down of a fence, and a degree of physical violence is almost irresistably attracted by sitting down on a highway.

Here then, from this more detailed sketch of CND in its youth and now in its adulthood, is the evidence without which the programmes of peacemakers in general and nuclear disarmers in particular would appear presumptuous. My own conviction is that they confirm the pacifist case. Its idealism turns out to be realistic.

Underlying all the other major and minor differences between the CND campaigns of the sixties and eighties, lies this absolute issue. To what extent, if at all, can mass violence of any kind, but pre-eminently by armed forces, be successfully used in the prosecution of peace?

Here are the answers which I believe must be drawn from this evidence. The inability of CND to become a successful mass movement that would, in fact, transform events was due to the increasing uncertainty of a world where certain types of weapons had been renounced but others were to be tolerated if not welcomed — after all Aldermaston was associated with other forms of mass violence than nuclear. The distinction between the capacity and indiscriminate use of nuclear warheads as compared with the atomic bombs dropped on Hiroshima, is a question of quantity rather than quality. The insistence on nuclear rather than total disarmament impoverishes the moral basis of peacemaking. The use of mass violence is not half bad and half good. It is all bad and only an outright repudiation will suffice in the eighties.

Finally, in the new and growing campaign of this CND, and especially among the Greenham Common women, I find not only something which in principle I wholeheartedly support, but also a number of problems which were by no means absent from the CND of the fifties, but have become more acute and immediate today.

There are few more important maxims for the would-be peacemaker than, 'If at first you don't succeed, try, try, and try again'. Indeed, I have been trying, however imperfectly, for more than fifty years. We did not succeed in the thirties. We did not succeed in the fifties. We have not succeeded yet in the eighties. There are three possible reasons for this non-success: it was not on the cards anyhow; we have not tried hard enough; we need to change our methods.

The Greenham Common saga is supremely significant at this point. CND began in demonstrations, it fostered propaganda, and it called attention through all kinds of dramatic events to the cause it advocated. When its effectiveness diminished it found no substitute for these methods apart from sporadic forays into more physical practices such as included the first 'sit-ins'.

Whether from desperation or from profounder commitment or because 'try, try, and try again' seems to be an unrewarding piece of advice, the Greenham Common women have mingled a certain violence to physical objects such as fences, with actions calculated to evoke a more or less violent response. Sitting in comfort writing these words, I have nothing but contempt for those critics who accuse them of Trotskyist methods and I have great respect for the

64

overwhelming majority of women who are demonstrating at Greenham Common for the unilateral rejection of nuclear arms as a stage in the rejection of all forms of mass violence. Yet, quite apart from the compromise with certain forms of violence itself, which I understand but cannot support, I believe that even this degree of violence is pragmatically a hindrance rather than a help. Once again, the assault on violence suffers from a loss of credibility when some of the weapons in that assault are of the same character, though certainly not of the same calibre, as those used against them.

The media have been able to asperse the overall integrity of the Greenham Common women's peaceful intention, by concentrating on the occasional mayhem that accompanies the attempt to tear down the fences and forcibly occupy, if possible, the heartland of the base itself.

Perhaps the most remarkable of the exploits of Gandhi was his ability to purge his campaigns from any contamination of violence as to make it quite impossible, except by downright lies, to sully the programme of Satyagraha. Greenham Common reminds me of Gandhi's own description of the word:

> Satyagraha is referred to in English as passive resistance and denotes the method of securing rights by personal suffering. I use the term 'soul force'. For example, the government of the day has passed a law which is applicable to me. I do not like it. If, by using violence, I force the government of the day to repeal the law, I am employing body force as violence. If I do not obey the law and accept the penalty for breaking it, I use soul force.

Such pacifism is a refinement of moral behaviour to which I aspire and increasingly feel committed, however far short of its heights I struggle.

So, almost with reluctance, I find the various activities and the mixed reception accorded to the brave women of Greenham Common, a further confirmation that nothing short of pacifism which opposes violence with a total repudiation in so far as any individual in this war-soaked human climate is a free agent, will finally work.

To 'try, try, and try again' is not enough. Peace on Earth, as I still hope for it and believe in it, awaits the trying for the first time in the rest of the developed world the experience that Gandhi undertook in the underdeveloped Eastern one.

CHAPTER SEVEN

For lo! the days are hastening on,
By prophet bards foretold,
When with the ever-circling years
Comes round the age of gold.
When peace shall over all the earth
Its ancient splendours fling,
And the whole world give back the song
Which now the angels sing.

The hymn is 'It Came Upon A Midnight Clear', and I have been singing it at every Christmas since I can first remember. It is a good tune and, like Proust's 'Snatch From Vertueil', the words and tune are 'encrusted with the pearls of nostalgia'. But now in the 1980s I can no longer enjoy it with the innocent acceptance of my early years. The nagging thought of its credibility becomes an urgent and demanding challenge, for I have long since been dissatisfied with its circular view of history. The years do not revolve, and there is no paradisical past to which we look back with longing and also with the expectation of its recurrence.

But what of the splendours of peace in which the song of God's Heavenly Host is to be echoed in the lives of God's earthly children? After two thousand years, it is no longer possible to rebuke ourselves for impatience, or to confront ourselves with the Christian equivalent of 'Next year in Jerusalem'.

There are, of course, theological arguments designed to keep our hopes high, but they are spiritual whistlings in the dark of dogma rather than in any light of reason. The most familiar is the confidence that peace will be established by divine fiat which completely by-passes the human condition. Quite apart from its basic improbability, it would, were it a true assessment, raise the all-important question as to whether a loving God ought not to have issued this fiat ages ago, thereby rescuing His creatures from the miseries caused by their violence and perpetuated by their impotence to overcome it.

Another hope lies in the promise that reassures the believer in peace only by separating its achievement from time and reserving it for eternity. But the express promise was Peace on Earth and no anticipations of peace beyond our earthly experiences can be introduced as a substitute for this here and now proclamation.

For those who are not to be satisfied with these theological rationalizations, the question remains – is Peace on Earth credible? I believe that the evidence yielded by the various personal episodes I have described, although it comes not from two thousand years but from no more than sixty years, provides valuable inferences if not answers to this question which is now the more urgent of human problems.

I find that in none of the periods in my lifetime that I have described, is there any substantial evidence that the prospect of peace has increased in any essential way. What is more, I find myself wondering why this bleak prognosis could have been ignored for so long in my own experience, and why it has found so little space in the published thoughts of Christian thinkers who have considered the Gospel as good news rather than good advice.

I suppose that there have been times when universal peace seemed a reasonable proposition. In a world which hardly extended beyond the Mediterranean, particularly when in the heyday of the Roman domination a kind of baptized *'pax romana'* held sway, it must have been an acceptable belief. Had those who cherished such a confidence about the future been in possession of the brute facts of the New World across the Atlantic, and the Goths and Ostrogoths and Visigoths beyond their Holy Roman Empire, it would have been a very different story.

One of the permanent effects of the capture of Constantinople by the infidel Ottoman Turks was to put an effective end to the idea of a peaceful apocalypse, in the same way that the passing of the year 1000 without unusual incident destroyed the belief in a spiritual one.

Another historical example of peace expectation can be associated with the heyday of the *'pax brittanica'* in the late nineteenth century. To the idea of the British Empire as a worldwide expression of social harmony, the missionary enthusiasm of the Western Churches added the equally confident expectation of the triumph of the Christian religion. By the time I was reading *With the Flag to Pretoria*, the emptiness of this sense of an impending era of consummation was already being tacitly accepted, if not intelligently understood. The plain fact was that the first quarter of the twentieth century was to become riddled with a mass of violence comparable to any previous period since the first Christmas and, in quantity if not in quality, it was unprecedented.

In retrospect, a fact which now is as clear as then it was not, neither in the Church (which, as I have said, was my second home) nor on any peace movement was I exposed to any counter-propaganda to the obsessive acceptance of a war climate. I realize now that there was a War Resisters International and there were Quakers. Yet for me, at that most impressionable age, there was practically nothing to counteract the assumption that war was an integral element in the world in which I was living. There appeared no practical equivalent for war. A world of peace was as far off as it must have appeared to the shepherds of old in their occupied country. It was not seriously entertained.

Turning now to the inter-war years, I can see with hindsight that, alongside the unsolved problem of a practical equivalent for a wartime climate, there existed an equally disabling absence of what has since been widely recognized as the 'moral' equivalent for war. The Peace Pledge Union testified to the need for a morality that could outdo in fervour and resilience the moral qualities (and of course there are many of them, like courage and sacrifice) that belong to soldiering. Unfortunately, it also testified to the need for a spiritual and intellectual depth in that morality which, as it turned out, was not sufficient for the task that 'War We Say No' set itself. This remains true even when it can be argued that those years included a higher quality of peacemaking than in almost any other period in which ordinary people revolted against the entire practice of violence or yearned for a different and nobler way of life.

I can remember Brigadier Crozier, who had known the horrors of the Black and Tans in Ireland, insisting on the need to harness the soldierly qualities of which he was an admirable example to another

68

kind of warfare. But even at the height of the campaign for that nobler warfare — the writing was on the wall. There was not enough moral or practical dynamism to arrest the slide to 1939 and the Second World War.

In that area of existence which is governed by human behaviour, the optimistic idea of an evolutionary progress working towards eventual peace, simply does not seem to apply. The human species appears to be incorrigibly violent. The Marxist argues that we should accept this hypothesis and channel this violence, use it as an instrument to transform society so profoundly that future generations may be able to live without war. The Christian refuses, or should refuse, to accept this hypothesis, because it has continued to hold sway in the absence of a more dominant power than violence itself. That greater power is non-violent love, and it must surely be agreed that the story so far is of failure to secure Peace on Earth by any other means.

Non-violent love has not been tried and found wanting — it has been found difficult and not tried. So just as the word 'evolution' is inapplicable so the word 'revolution' is relevant both for Marxists and for would-be Christians alike. I cannot accept the Marxist recipe for future peace as the product of the violent overthrow of the present warmongering society. It manifestly has demonstrated since 1917 in the Soviet Union that, far from the end justifying the means, the means determine the end. You can do anything with a bayonet except sit on it.

I shall here endeavour to set out what is the Christian programme of action that can revolutionize an age-long situation of mass violence, which has hitherto been impervious to any other method of restraining it. It is the creed and practice of pacifism to which I have already adverted. It aspires to a total life style. Whatever the elements of approximation that are inevitable in an imperfect world in respect of many desirable causes of action (for example the impossibility of a socialist avoiding all actions that directly or indirectly contribute to a capitalist system), the pacifist, so far as he is a free agent, must refuse to be violent or to support violence whatever the circumstances. For those interested in the theological argument on this issue, there can in the matter of violence be no such principle as a 'situational ethic' — that is, that a moral principle varies according to the circumstances in which it is expected to apply. In practical terms, the absolute pacifist position must be

69

maintained in defiance of even situations where the immediate effect of such consistency may well seem completely unreasonable if not disastrous.

The classic example of this problem lies in the sort of question with which I have been confronted a hundred times at Hyde Park. What would you do if some thug attacked your wife? It is a genuine question and there is nothing so unworthy as to dodge it by suggesting that he does not know my wife. There is, on the other hand, something to be said for pointing out the difficulty of giving a specific answer to a general question. What was the locale of the supposed attack? Was anybody else about at the time? Wouldn't both of you run away? Nonetheless, whatever the 'consequential' argument may be, I submit that the only kind of non-violence that can generate a revolutionary power sufficient to supplant the power of naked force, is the non-violence that remains loyal to its fundamental requirement under any and every circumstance. In this particular, hypothetical case, that intention must be accompanied by the candid admission that I can give no absolute assurance that I would have the moral guts to practise what I preach. I would, I hope, be ready to interpose my body between my wife and the attacker.

The fact is that the moral dynamic of the entire pacifist case is not invalidated until every hypothetical emergency has been covered. This is all the more apposite when the violence is mass violence. The objective is to create the degree of moral power sufficient, as I have argued, to defeat the powers inherent in the kind of society in which hitherto we all have lived. This, I contend, can only be done by a total repudiation of violence, however apparently foolhardy in the personal field, together with a condition of total disarmament in the corporate one. Just as the private act of renunciation must be unilateral, so unilateral action in the matter of disarmament must be the guiding principle. Multilateral action to reduce or eliminate weaponry carries with it no necessary moral dynamic. Furthermore, the idea that countries armed to the teeth and profoundly suspicious of one another will one bright morning simultaneously acknowledge a common impulse to disarm, is, I submit, a psychological monstrosity. The tale of disarmament conference after conference professing multilateral aims is that they have foundered because such aims required the initial action to get the disarmament talks off the ground, and no party to the conference was prepared, unilaterally, to set such action in train.

70

Moreover, the limited aims of disarmers – the repudiation of specific weapons, nuclear or chemical, thus leaving other weapons at that stage intact – suffers from a similar lack of moral thrust. No country tells the truth about its armoury and, in the fog of mutual mistrust and deceit, the weapons that are excluded from the proscribed list may constitute almost as great a threat to peace as the mutual abandonment of the more horrible weapons which are assumed to minimize that threat.

Those who oppose nuclear disarmament on the grounds that it will make 'conventional' warfare more likely, should not be written off as puerile. They have a case, but the real objection to a concentration of effort on the mutual abandonment of the more horrendous instruments of destruction is that, like multilateralism, it does not generate the moral fervour that total disarmament could achieve.

So if, on reflection and out of my own experience, I ask myself, 'Is peace on earth worth cherishing as a good that can be reached?' my answer must be that it is, but only if there can be introduced into the human arena, which until now gives little or no evidence that such a good is possible, a superior kind of power than peacemaking up to now has been able to mobilize.

For me, that power is the pacifism I have endeavoured very imperfectly to outline. This is the road to Peace on Earth, but the promise of real peace proclaimed at the first Christmas was linked with two other proclamations, Goodwill Among Men and Glory to God in the Highest. The foregoing advocacy of pacifism, however sound its argument and desirable its application, needs to be set within the framework of a just society and the authority of the Divine Purpose if its power is to become good news instead of the best of good advice. If the one hope, the one just reaction for that optimism is the discovery and practice of the power of non-violence, it must operate in the actual conditions that we call political and economic.

I turn now, therefore, to a consideration of the meaning of Goodwill Among Men as the second element in the optimistic outlook for humankind.

Part Two
Goodwill Among Men

CHAPTER EIGHT

I INTEND TO use this promise of Goodwill Among Men announced by the 'multitude of the Heavenly Host', unashamedly as a gate into the field of the social gospel. The Goodwill in the authorized version of the Bible is the proclamation of a human condition to which man can move because it is the will of God. In the revised version, and in other translations, the Goodwill is that will of God in which peace is not only the overthrow of violence but the positive tranquillity and well-being which can take the place of that violence. The Kingdom of Heaven is infinitely worth seeking as the redeemed society from which man has been expelled because of his disobedience and which he can re-attain. The Sermon on the Mount expresses beyond any peradventure that to seek that Kingdom and its righteousness is the first and imperative requirement of Christian discipleship.

So in as much as man is a social animal the good news is essentially a social gospel, which is a condition of the life here on earth being enjoyed by God's creatures in whom, as the revised version has it, 'God is well pleased', or as I heard expressed in a sermon the other day, 'benevolently orientated'.

As in the realm of peacemaking, I will endeavour to call up experiences and episodes in my life and ministry which have been concerned with that social gospel. What is the practical nature of that good news as it applies to politics and economics? And what are the prospects of final success in the quest for the Kingdom of God on this earth and in our time? These are the key issues which are prompted by the recall of past experiences.

It happened in Derby. I was a student in my second year at Cambridge and, under the auspices of the Student Christian Movement, was taking part in an evangelical campaign. I realize now how unfitted I was for such activities but my personal commitment to Christianity was real, and I declared it along with others in the Derby Market Place.

Later, we were offered the opportunity of visiting the railway works which were and still are one of the principal local industries. Having only recently emerged from years which were cloistered not only by the fact that I was at school, but by the isolating effect of the First World War, I had had no direct experience of a factory in full blast. The immediate effect of my confrontation with a world of noise and dirt and machinery and, above all, human workers was as sudden as it was inexplicable in rational terms. The experience had all the ingredients and power of a religious conversion. It was a 'second birth', since I became vividly aware of a life of which previously I had known nothing. It was a 'revelation', incomplete of course, but self-authenticating in the sense that it seemed to preclude any doubt. In that brief excursion into the world of industry, I had a direct experience of a truth vouchsafed to me for the first time, which demanded a radical change of mental and moral direction. I do not claim any particular merit for what happened in that Derby factory, but as I think about it and live it again in retrospect, I can feel its vividness and its intensity. It was a new beginning – of that I have no doubt.

I had thought of Goodwill Among Men as a sort of personal relationship in which losing one's temper would be replaced by meekness of spirit, malevolence towards others would give way to friendliness of heart, and we would love our neighbour as we loved ourselves. Now there is nothing wrong with these moral aims except that they set Goodwill within far too simplistic and narrow a context. That revelation in a factory in Derby was the sudden recognition of the lawyer's question in the Parable of the Good Samaritan: 'Who is my neighbour?' It is not just my fellow man any more than the Samaritan was just the 'fellow man' of the one who 'fell among thieves'. Like the Jew and the Samaritan, those factory workers and we undergraduates belonged to two, almost entirely different, economic and political and probably social worlds.

It was not as if my mind had not already concerned itself with political theories or economic matters. I was reading for the first part of the History Tripos. I had also in 1924 been a delegate to the conference known as COPEC (Conference on Politics, Economics and Citizenship), chiefly promoted by the great Dr William Temple. I remember him announcing from the chair that, of all the world's religions, Christianity was the most materialistic. Even then, it appeared to me to be a reasonable thing to say, although it put a theological cat among any number of religious pigeons. What came to me now with all the authority of conviction was that social politics and personal ethics were the obverse and reverse of the same model. Goodwill was not a private, moral condition that had to be applied to a variety of public issues. It was at one and the same time an attitude to one's neighbour and to one's neighbourhood, and the second was not merely a corollary of the first.

I have been asked a thousand times since that day in Derby why, as a professing Christian, I spend so much time, especially in the open air, talking about politics, the assumption being that this is an unworthy and irrelevant use of the preacher's time. I try to answer by saying that, if I am concerned – as I should be – to advocate such a change in our affairs as will bring us close to God's purposes and promises, then politics is largely the way such things happen. Indifference, or indeed hostility to the arena where the action is taking place, is the single most damaging accusation that is levelled at so much of contemporary churchmanship.

As a disgruntled heckler once said on Tower Hill: 'The trouble with you parsons is that you are everlastingly answering the questions no one is asking.' The accusation may be extravagant, but it contains an element of truth – a concentration on matters which are exclusively 'spiritual' has time and again been the occupational disease of the pulpiteer. All too often the Church has assumed a concern about eternal life on the part of its congregations when, as a matter of bare fact, the cares of this world have rendered such a preoccupation practically impossible.

Paradoxically enough, the net result of this indifference to material and immediate needs has been to offer to the economically hopeless and helpless a spurious contentment in the next world, to compensate for the total inability to find the Kingdom of God here and now. Perhaps the classic example of this transference of hope from one world to the next is to be found in the negro spiritual. Within the simplicity and realism of the words, there lies a belief that Christianity can say very little about the possible emancipation of the slave but everything about his dignity and place in the next world. 'I got shoes, you got shoes, all God's children got shoes, when I get to heaven going to put on my shoes and going to walk all over God's heaven'. I have sung these words many a time and, while their beauty and humanity never fail to move me, the melancholy fact is that they represent an attitude to the Kingdom of God which is totally inadequate and which does not in fact reflect the spirit and teaching of Jesus. No wonder religion has been described as the 'opium of the people'.

To realize that the Kingdom of God, the spirit of Goodwill on Earth, must be established in a locomotive factory if it is to belong to the real world, was indeed to me a sudden conversion. If to conclude that I entered that factory a political illiterate and came out a convinced socialist, is an over-simplification, it is true to say that the experience illuminated for me a pathway.

Goodwill Among Men came to me as a vision of a far horizon. If the freshness of that view were difficult to descry, it was nevertheless a vision which captivated me. Its outline was clear and it was a pleasant land, a promised land. At the same time, I recognized that gazing into the distance can quickly degenerate into a fantasy unless the view can be sufficiently foreshortened to provide as clear an outline of the possible road to that horizon as the horizon itself. With a mixture of impatience, and what I would presume to think was insight, that road became recognizable and available. The road was socialism and, since that time, I have never found any reason to reject that association of the Kingdom of God and the socialist ideology.

The implication, particularly on economic terms, of this interdependence of a religious gospel and a political programme, was for me a long way off and I can suitably describe that development later on. What is pertinent to this stage in my thinking is the fact that the political and economic policies and programmes, to which I later found myself committed, were the outcome of a conversion rather than the product of an academic course of study. This meant that, however inadequately I acted in the political arena, for me politics and economics were, from the first, sacramental rather than utilitarian.

Lest the use of that word 'sacramental' in this context be regarded as impious, I ought to explain what the word conveys to me. A sacrament is an act of process in the ordinary world which is the

78

symbol or reminder of a deeper spiritual meaning. For example, the act of breaking and eating a piece of bread at the service of Holy Communion is the symbol of the breaking of the bread of life itself to nourish the creatures of God. More intimately, it serves to remind the believer that that bread which he eats signifies the body of the saviour of the world by whose spirit every meal must be a sharing of God's bounty and love. In that meaning of sacrament, commerce and industry, wages and profits, the Acts of Parliament, and the rule books of the trades union must become the expressions and the symbols of ideas which go far beyond their immediate significance.

The setting of the issue of Goodwill Among Men in the frame of a sudden and vital awareness carries with it two consequences for me, and indeed for many of my contemporaries. They are, I would argue, general regulative principles in the quest for that Goodwill and are as relevant today as when first they impressed themselves on me and my fellow students. The first was the awareness that quickly accompanies any attempt to visualize Goodwill in human affairs of a ratio between the complexity of those affairs and the difficulty of putting that Goodwill into effect. This apparent platitude is at the heart of the failure during the 1920s and 1930s to maintain the impetus of enthusiasm for a better world. As in the quest for peace, so in the pursuit of social justice, weariness in well-doing is the product of a previous exhaustion. We can be so tired out with the effort to conceive of that justice in areas of ever-increasing social complexity, that we have no energy left to pursue it.

The second regulative principle embedded in many ways follows on from the first and is the answer to it — or at least it was in my case. A vision, that is a prospect which catches the imagination, does not need at the outset a rational foundation in order to validate it, but it will quickly turn into a mirage unless reason invests that vision with practicality. The socialism which began for me as a sort of compelling vision would have rapidly degenerated into an unreal dream without the realization that Goodwill demands a platform as well as a pulpit.

The preacher in the old Methodist chapels stood high up above his congregation as he offered the good news, but he had to come down sooner or later to a much lower level if that good news was to be turned to practical effect. What had often seemed to deter preachers from stepping down from the pulpit was that the platform represented not only a lower profile but a much more restricted one.

79

So it is. Politics is the art of the possible and even if that art is seen in the light of the ideal, a great deal of it has to be undertaken on a wobbling easel, with restricted colours and inadequate brushes.

Coming to terms with the practical solution alongside the spiritual vision marked a definite stage in my ministry. I came to see how impossible it is to funnel the Christian message through one outlet. The preacher who endeavours to cram everything he wants to say into his Sunday sermon will find himself attempting a two-fold task at one and the same time. Worship, prayer and the fellowship of believing cannot satisfactorily be combined with the demands of practical discipleship and political responsibility in the same sermon, however protracted. The secret of a successful ministry is the discovery and use of the platform which does not take the place of the pulpit but complements it. How fortunate I was to discover this so early, and then for fifty years to occupy a pulpit at 11am on Sunday and to stand on a platform at 3pm the same day.

However badly I fulfilled that ministry, I am profoundly grateful for the opportunity to offer a full Gospel of prayer and practice separated in location but, I hope, blended in effect. The planks in that platform were for me shaped by the public events of the 1920s and 1930s.

In 1926 occurred the General Strike. Historians now agree that the immediate reason why the strikers went back to work was the appeal on the part of Mr Baldwin the Prime Minister to a spirit of goodwill. Even while this appeal was having its effect, it was becoming equally evident that none of the fundamental issues which had caused this industrial crisis had been resolved, any more than they had been seriously appreciated. With a number of friends I had attended a meeting of strikers a few miles from Cambridge, and had been left in no doubt that the whole structure of the society in which they and we were obliged to live was inimical to Goodwill. Political and economic changes were imperative if a mood of Goodwill were to turn into a permanent process of friendliness and mutual cooperation.

This somewhat inchoate socialism not only required a political scaffolding if there were to be any appreciable progress towards a solution of the underlying evils of the system in which the General Strike was taking place, but it also required a set of proposals capable of being put into immediate effect, and an organization both committed to those proposals and organized to implement them. In short, more than simply an awareness of political issues was needed. What was implied from that first visit to the Derby factory all the way to the acceptance of involvement in the field of politics, is the application of the Gospel, and the necessary road to the fulfilment of the Christian message of Goodwill was the fact that politics must be party politics if it is to become the machinery of Goodwill on Earth.

I recognized from the first that the Labour Party was not committed in every respect to the socialism which I was seeking to embrace, and I could see the extent to which it had grown up as an opposition to powers entrenched within the capitalist system. Nevertheless, I believed then, as now, that what I cherished was possible within its framework. I became convinced that there was within this party the innate possibility of the socialism which I wanted to see, and therefore I found no sense of unworthy compromise in giving my allegiance, such that it was, to party politics.

I joined the Labour Party.

CHAPTER NINE

IF THERE IS ONE place, more than any other, that calls to mind the dominant aspect of my working life, it must be a wall. It is the boundary of a cobbled area on what is called Tower Hill. Prisoners from the Tower of London were executed there in past days. In more recent times, since the great London docks' strike of 1889, it has become an open-air forum like Speakers' Corner in Hyde Park, but confined to middays and frequented by office workers and dock workers in their lunch hour. What part that wall came to play in my life began with two coincidences, one in time and the other in place.

In 1926, my last year at theological college, the newly-opened Wesley House at Cambridge, I was told by my spiritual superiors that my first appointment as a probationary minister would be the Methodist Mission House, where I was to be responsible for some very modest aspects of the world mission of Methodism. But on the very day that I was to take my final examination in Part Two of the Theological Tripos, I was informed that this appointment had fallen through. I could have wished that the authorities had chosen a rather more suitable time to disturb my ecclesiastical prospects, but I had no choice in the matter.

It was over a month later that I was in London's Old Kent Road, posted to a church known locally as the one between the Dun Cow and the Duke of Wellington. I found myself suddenly confronted with an area of poverty and much destitution, and indeed with the challenge of the socialism I had so recently embraced. Had I not been appointed to this church in the London Mission, it is highly unlikely that the second coincidence would have followed.

One of the young men in the congregation told me that, at a place called Tower Hill, he had been listening to speakers who seemed to believe that Christianity was a lot of nonsense, and he raised a number of questions in the hope that I could answer them. Before endeavouring to do so, I suggested that I should go with him to Tower Hill. I had no intention of doing more than getting to know the sort of open-air meetings at which he had been troubled by these doubts. We went together the next day.

There were a number of meetings in progress: a huckster was trying to sell Californian pine oil as a cure-all, and an escapologist was extracting himself from a number of very rusty chains. I stood by a wall and listened for a while. Then I remember saying to someone sitting on the wall: 'How do you start a meeting?'

'Stand up on the wall and they'll come,' he replied. 'If they don't, clap your hands.' I did as he suggested and soon quite a crowd gathered. I announced that I was a parson and that I would answer the kind of questions that the crowd might care to ask. I stood there on a quite sudden impulse, nervous but at the same time confident that my theological training would provide me with the answers to whatever questions might be thrown at me.

I was quickly undeceived. The first question I was asked was about Karl Marx. Although I was soon to start reading for my Doctorate in Philosophy at the London School of Economics, Marx was no more than a name to me at that time and I was almost totally ignorant of what he had written. In all my training in church history, biblical doctrine, theological dogmas, moral principles, he and what he stood for had never been introduced either as friend or foe. I therefore told the questioner that I would not want to give him a hasty answer but that I would come back with the answer the next week. I rambled on for a little while, but that initial adventure into field preaching was anything but a distinguished debut.

Returning home, I got in touch with one or two of my fellow ministers, but I have to record that they did not seem to have heard of Marx either. However, my Superintendent, the Reverend Roderick Kedward, who incidentally was for a time the Liberal MP for Bermondsey, came to my rescue with his own knowledge of communism and with a suggestion as to the sort of literature I needed to read on the subject. By the next Wednesday, I was at least able to carry on a more or less intelligent conversation about Marxism as the alternative answer to the Christian argument.

Looking back after fifty-seven years on that wall (although now

I'm too decrepit to balance on it so I use the stand of the Catholic Evidence Guild which is stored at the Church of All Hallows nearby — it is a kindly ecumenical gesture on their part), I can see that I have been doing it ever since. *

There were many other topics on which my knowledge was wholly as sketchy if not as bereft, as on my first encounter with Marxism. As the years went by and I also ventured into Hyde Park on Sunday afternoons and began to speak there some ten years after my first excursion to Tower Hill, this outdoor experience of Christian evangelism confirmed a number of lessons and impressions which, although they have deepened with time, were really there from the beginning. I would presume to say that the prospects of success, the quest for Goodwill Among Men, are linked with the acceptance of these lessons. To begin with, Christianity was born in the open air. The Sermon on the Mount was preached there, the arguments with the opponents of Jesus took place there, the hungry were fed there, the cross was set up there, and Jesus came back to Mary, his friend, in a garden. Again, Methodism was similarly born in the open air. It was the field preaching of Wesley and Whitefield which resulted in the revival of religion in England in the eighteenth century. It is surely not fanciful to believe that, once more, the open air may provide the favourable venue for evangelism today.

On the other hand, it would be fanciful to imagine that any pattern of Christian service only needs to be taken out of doors for it to succeed. The so-called 'hymn-sermon sandwich' is almost entirely unsuitable for the street corner — as the Salvation Army would now be prepared to acknowledge, and they have the advantage of skilled musicians playing exciting instruments. Moreover, there is obviously a powerful place for the open-air mass which, as an occasional large-scale celebration, has advertised the faith to the outside and offered comfort and reassurance to the faithful.

Essentially, the proclamation of the Christian faith out of doors is different from the other forms of advocacy. It is not conducted in a confined space. It is open-ended, as a service indoors is not. To come, to remain, to go, are entirely optional, whereas there is a degree of restraint that surrounds even the freest of public meetings within a building. In this sense, preaching in the open air is an

.* These matters are covered in more detail in my book, *Christ on Tower Hill* 12.30

uncomplicated undertaking – no limiting conventions, no protocol of procedure, no scaffolding of programme or 'Order of Service', no hymns and presumably no collection. It is speaking pure (that is, undiluted) and simple.

Moreover, in these islands, this sort of communication possesses a unique degree of 'freedom of speech'. The written word and nowadays the word from radio or television, are hedged with obvious or concealed restraints which invite a certain suspicion in the listener that the message is doctored before it is delivered. Whether this is always a worthy suspicion does not alter the fact that it can appear so, and therefore impair the impact of the message.

Is it too much to argue that, in the world of the media, places like Tower Hill and Speakers' Corner are the only truly free forum available for the ordinary citizen? From one standpoint, such a claim is incontrovertible. You can answer back in the open air and such a participation in the liturgy is immediate in a way that a letter to *The Times* cannot be. A malediction or the mildest of heckling in church is likely to be frowned upon as a disturbance of worship. This immediacy of the open air is, in my experience, of the utmost importance. The lack of it in evangelism generally provides the strongest evidence for the current failures in organized Christianity. In as much as the trend of argument in all fields is about what is true in the light of what we understand by the so-called scientific approach to reality (and five minutes at almost any discussion of almost any topic must surely confirm such a claim), coming to grips with this sort of urgency of controversy is the substance of the effective use of the soapbox.

Here, as nowhere else to the same degree, the speaker can be challenged to say what he means by the words he uses even as he utters those words. Similarly, the questioner can be required to explain what he means by his question before the speaker endeavours to answer it. Herein lies the directness of such debate as contrasted with the complete waste of time that invariably follows the failure to 'define one's terms'. Words may conceal thought, and to take a term like socialism and argue with three or four other people as to its desirability while each one of the arguers has a different meaning of the word at the back of his mind, and no attempt is made to define it, is a recipe for disaster. On the other hand, the patient, persistent attempt to get behind the words to the issues which they are assumed to represent, can constitute one of the most effective means of education and influence in whatever area of human activity. In the endeavour to promote Peace on Earth, this sort of forum, which encourages the kind of fellowship of controversy I have been describing, is indispensable and, on the whole, a reason for optimism.

One of the exciting differences between preaching from a pulpit to a congregation of the faithful and speaking in the open air, is that from time to time in Hyde Park your crowd includes, if only for a fleeting moment, quite famous people who would be highly unlikely to attend worship at, shall we say, Kingsway Hall. I particularly remember Jomo Kenyatta who for some months was a fairly regular member of the crowd and, somewhat to my surprise, an attentive and silent one. However, it is one thing to recognize a notability and to take suitable precautions in what you say, but quite another to find all too late that you have been expatiating on a theme with the impression that you are better acquainted with it than the crowd, only to find how insecure is such an assumption.

The most devastating example of that danger happened on Tower Hill. The topic of the day was Anglo-American relations and I was trying to give some background to the contemporary situation between the two countries. In the course of this exposition, I mentioned the Monroe Doctrine which established in the nineteenth century the principle associated with the name of the United States President who proclaimed it, and which rejected European interference in transatlantic affairs. A white-haired member of the audience presumed to criticize my explanation of the Doctrine and suggested that I had given it a rather imperfect and unfair description. I would have nothing of this and told him so. He made no further comment but as I got down from the wall he enquired as to my name. I told him and then asked for his. He said that his name would not interest me, but he was a US Supreme Court judge and it was in that capacity that he had thought fit to make his observations on a matter of which he was professionally an authority. I could have wished that the ground had opened up. I was all the more ashamed when I recognized the courtesy with which he had refrained from exposing my ignorance to the crowd. It was a lesson I have never forgotten and I am eternally grateful to that judge. He has saved me over the years from similar disasters which might have happened had I not had that traumatic experience in the background of my mind ever since.

86

This was not the first of these practical illustrations of the underlying kindliness of a crowd which can appear in the heat of debate to be hostile and even malevolent. Some three years after I began on Tower Hill, I was dilating on the blessings and on the responsibilities of married life and giving advice to a questioner as to the resolution of a particular problem that worried him, when an old docker, who was a constant thorn in my side, wondered whether I was married and, when I said I was not, suggested that I did not know what I was talking about. This, in principle, I had to admit, but added that I was hoping to put the matter right as I was to be married in a fortnight's time.

Nothing more was said on that Wednesday, but a week later I was presented with a silver teapot filled with coins as a wedding present. The spokesman who handed it to me was a persistent heckler, and the good wishes that accompanied this present were voiced by a communist, a fervent agnostic, as well as all sorts of people who, in my limited experience of human nature, had given little evidence up to that point of such kindliness.

Mind you, one of them warned me that if ever I married again I could expect no second teapot. I have never had the slightest desire to do so. My marriage to Marie Dean, in 1929, was the best thing I ever did, and that silver teapot down the years has remained the symbol not only of the decency of an open-air crowd, but of the lasting happiness of a marriage rooted in the love of a wonderful and long-suffering wife. The experience of being, in the well-worn phrase, a family man – our four daughters Ann, Bridget, Judith and Caroline were born between 1931 and 1946 – made a world of difference to my thinking and outlook, and constituted a new dimension to my life as a whole.

I learnt another lesson from that first occasion on Tower Hill, which not only improved my education but contained a much more general truth. How does the speaker begin if there is no call to worship, no introductory prayer, and none of the symbols that will act as a frame for his message? There are gimmicks, more or less disreputable, which are called in – principally, I should add, by secular speakers in the open air. Announce your intention to march on Buckingham Palace, as I remember one such speaker proclaim as his immediate project, and you may well attract an immediate crowd, but the effect is ephemeral. To tell a funny story may attract attention, but somehow funny stories have little survival value in

87

Hyde Park. In fact, the most effective beginning is the simplest. Say something of topical interest, meeting your prospective audience where they are and not where you hope they will be. There is nothing unworthy in entering the discussion through this mundane door, although I still meet fervent Christians who insist that the speaker is wilfully ignoring his true calling if he soils his message with political or economic matters.

Of course, evangelism in a setting where the heckler is lying in wait can be an exhilarating and a dangerous exercise. On one occasion I was arguing the temperance cause on Tower Hill and advocating total abstinence when a heckler intervened to ask whether I was not contradicting the Scriptures. After all, did not Paul advocate 'a little wine for thy stomach's sake?' I told him with what assurance I could command that, if Paul did say so he certainly meant rub it in rather than take it by any other means. The heckler persisted, even after I tried to tell him that it was extremely dangerous to use quotations from the Bible because you could find a quotation to suit almost any case. To prove it, I countered his quotation from Paul with one from the Book of Proverbs, which said: 'Wine is a mocker, strong drink is raging for at the last it biteth like a serpent and stingeth like an adder'. The man replied that he had been looking for that kind of stuff for the past ten years. I hardly believe the cause of temperance was advanced on that Wednesday.

That first open-air question about Marx was significant in two ways. It set the pattern of the meeting. It started a discussion, albeit short-lived on that first occasion, rather than introducing a speech. The to and fro of verbal controversy is the life-blood of open-air speaking. It is precluded by the use of the loud speaker which almost invariably turns the occasion on which it is used into a demonstration rather than a conversation. I have never known a time on Tower Hill when an issue or topic in the morning newspaper could not start an argument, and incidentally arguing is an infectious condition. Start with one person and others will be affected by the very atmosphere of the occasion. The secret of the initial discussion is to be able to use it in order to interpret the deeper significance behind the particular question in a climate of interest. If that deeper significance had preceded it instead of growing out of it, the message would have fallen upon uninterested ears and probably on no ears at all. Most people can be superficially stimulated by reference to the everyday problems that vex them. It is best of all for the speaker if the problem is initiated from the crowd rather than the soapbox.

If the open-air speaker is prepared intelligently and honestly to face such matters, he stands a reasonable chance of gathering and holding an audience. He must, of course, use his voice and not abuse it, but most voices can perform adequately out of doors with a bit of help. It is equally important that a speaker should look relatively happy in his work. Decent people, very properly, are disinclined to watch somebody suffering.

Of one thing I am certain. Open-air speaking reflects the old rule: 'You never know what you can do till you try'. I wish many more ministers of religion would try. I would go so far as to say that the future well-being of our modern society is bound up with the sort of public occasion which stretches from the Athenian *agora* right through to Hyde Park on a Sunday afternoon.

The other significance of that original question about Karl Marx lies in the background of ideas from which it emerged. It was now, as for millions of my generation, that Marx exploded on my consciousness like a bomb the moment I was compelled to read about him rather than refer to him in passing as one of the non-Christian thinkers in the modern world. Marxism immediately struck me not so much with its dialectic structure, its theory of value, its concept of the proletarian role and its dynamic materialism, but with the total nature of its 'scientific' analysis, the claim to provide an answer to all the questions, which introduced into my own thinking a new dimension. Disturbingly, it forced me to realize that, if up to then I had begun to understand that politics is the way things happen in the light of an idea, I had now to take on board the Marxist theory that economics is the way things happen in the light of a determinist realism.

I find it almost impossible to recover exactly the frame of mind that coming to study Marx and Lenin and Trotsky imposed anew upon my thinking, because I now recollect it through the looking-glass of almost half a century in which I must have listened to thousands of hours of debate and spoken myself many thousands of words in argument about Marxist theory and practice. In one respect that initial impression has remained inviolate. Whether or not economics (that is, the way human beings behave in their everyday life) is the key to everything, from the basic struggle to survive to the superstructure of art and religion, it undoubtedly plays a dominant role in our lives. Goodwill, therefore must take economic matters into the most serious account. To ignore this fact or to denigrate it is escapist or irrelevant.

My first excursion to Tower Hill made me question with a new urgency whether until now in my ministry I had been doing little more than making pious noises in peculiar places. I had to make more articulate noises in more familiar places, and this turned out to be much more like a baptism of fire on a most dangerous and unreconnoitred battlefield.

CHAPTER TEN

As ONE OF John Wesley's travelling preachers, I must confess to a certain sluggishness. For the last fifty years I have had only one appointment and that has been to the London Mission of the Methodist Church, first in the Old Kent Road, then for seven years in Islington, and for the rest of the time at Kingsway Hall and Hinde Street Church. It would be difficult to recall, in this long apprenticeship to a city ministry, one episode which would bring to life all its essential nature. Nonetheless, of all the activities and occasions of so many years, there is one which is redolent of the characteristic flow of most of the others and is, for me, unforgettable. It concerns some tired vegetables.

At the height of the blitz, I received a telephone call from the Ministry of Food. There was concern about conditions in Covent Garden Market where, due to the dislocation from the bombing, many vegetables were not being delivered to the consumer and were, as they put it, growing 'tired'. Would we in the West London Mission (because Kingsway Hall was only a few yards from Covent Garden) be prepared to distribute the said vegetables to people who needed them? We said, 'Yes'. The next problem was transport. So I rang the Ministry of Transport. The spokesman there was sympathetic but regretted that he was unable to help with the loan of a lorry or two. He asked my name again and when I told him wondered whether I was the same Soper with whom he had been at school. I told him I was, and we had a pleasant chat about old times. Finally, he said, 'Now how many lorries did you say you wanted?' We were in business and, in addition to the comfort we were able to bring to all sorts of people, there was the sense of real satisfaction that the carrying out of the project gave to the social workers in the West London Mission itself.

In considering the prospect of Goodwill on Earth, in so far as my experience as a social missioner is involved, I am satisfied that the right place to start is with that sense of real satisfaction in meeting ordinary people's ordinary needs. To ignore the meaning that can be attached to this kind of social service is to leave out of account the one factor that, again and again in my ministry, counteracts the feeling of pessimism about social problems generally. Quite simply, it is this aspect of Christian morality that needs no justification beyond itself. So let me flesh out this experience of realism, which has been a dominant element for me in a prolonged attempt to proclaim the Gospel in the inner city. It is, I suppose, the truth that lies behind the adage that 'virtue is its own reward', or the ontological argument in plain clothes. In other words, it seems to me to mean that the search for the Kingdom of God, the good society, the Goodwill Among Men, is a self-validating experience – that we would not be looking for it if it were not there to be found.

Various aspects of a social ministry, of which the tired vegetable venture is a classic example, may help to illustrate what I mean and what I have come to believe. First, the successes. It was in the West London Mission that the first children's crèche in London, and probably the first in the United Kingdom, was set up in 1888, where mothers could leave their children for twelve hours for fourpence. What began as a single pathway for the necessary care of children who otherwise would be at risk during the day, has now become a broad highway of responsible local government. The experiment contained within itself its practical as well as its moral justification. Much more recently, with others I have been concerned with the ever-increasing danger of alcoholism, and have attempted to provide a threefold method of reducing, if not eliminating, that danger: an initial medical drying-out process, a period of some custodial rehabilitation and finally, some kind of protected housing for the recovered alcoholic who can, at best, look forward to a permanent convalescence. Here success has proved valuable in itself but also, innate to the undertaking, has been the satisfaction of being part of a dynamic social process. My experience – and it is shared by most of those who devote themselves to good works – is that this sense of hopefulness and inward satisfaction is enjoyed too by those whose efforts towards goodwill have appeared not to succeed but to fail. I think of the efforts, made under my

92

sponsorship as Superintendent from 1936 onwards, to provide a hostel environment for delinquent youths of both sexes — efforts which fall into the second of the two classes to which I have referred.

The statistics over the years have been disappointing. The majority of these youngsters left our care more or less as they entered it. If we achieved an eight per cent success rate, even that figure was, in many cases, a temporary judgment. It was no comfort to us that similar hostels elsewhere fared no better. In our boys' hostel, the expectation of life in the hostel for the television set was about six weeks and it then disappeared with our guests who also went AWOL. Yet even here, there is room for optimism. Recently the success rate of the hostels has tended to increase for, as in so many of these enterprises, the quality of leadership of those who take on this work is a prime factor in the general welfare of those for whom we seek to care. I have nothing but admiration for the splendid men and women who take on these vocational tasks.

Yet it would be absurd to say that the social work which I inherited in 1936 in the West London Mission is more or less the same in 1984. There was a kind of hopeless misery about the stark and terrible poverty of those days, which no longer exists. To compare the photographs of the crèche children of the 1920s with even those of the 1960s, is to have visual confirmation of a great improvement in physical condition and, judging by the smiles on the faces of the latter, a change for the better in other ways as well. The welfare state of which we were in many cases the 'bell-wethers' has made a world of difference — and practically all of it to the good.

But with these achievements there have emerged new problems and new evils. For example, the break-up of family life which, in my experience as a social worker, is more frequent and disastrous than ever before, is not only *'post hoc'* to the family life previously exposed to privation and poverty but *'propter hoc'* — the better standard of living enjoyed is a significant factor. But despite the satisfaction and, in some cases, success derived from social work of this kind, there is no place for complacency. I find it impossible and therefore dishonest, to derive from a lifetime's involvement in the field of service convincing evidence that the song of the Heavenly Host is much nearer fulfilment than it was when that song was first heard two thousand years ago. Furthermore, I find the so-called evidence of successive proponents of an earthly paradise, whether guaranteed by divine or human agencies, unsatisfying.

It must always be the aim of the social worker to identify as far as possible with the work which he undertakes. This is no easy task and, in one sense, it is an impossible one. I was trying to identify myself with people living in deprivation and poverty and experiencing all kinds of problems which I did not have to face. Although my life as a family man was by no means as continuous as for some others, yet I was blessed with a loving wife and family, and a comfortable home. This relative ease inevitably produced tensions now and then. Nevertheless, I believe that it is not inconsistent with such a ministry to cherish the opportunities and blessings of a happy family life and, at the same time, devote oneself to the office and the vocation of social care. However imperfectly I was able to fulfil this double way of life, I certainly believe that to be able to find rest, recreation and indeed blessing as husband and father did not imperil the sincerity of the vocation to which I was committed.

This inescapable commitment of a Methodist minister trying to do his job in the Old Kent Road or Islington or Kingsway not only confirmed the sense of satisfaction that, spiritually, it was the vocation to which I was called. At the same time, there was the irresistible feeling that such social work led inevitably to a commitment to the political and economic ideas I was then discovering. For me, Christian social work was the road to socialism. There is a 'pattern for living', an ideal plan for our human community. To be engaged in good works, even of a rescue nature, reminds the social worker of that pattern and tends to comfort him with the belief that he is becoming part of it. Realizing the limitations and frustrations that are part of that engagement challenges the social worker to examine the pattern more closely so that he may become a more effective agent in its fulfilment.

So I had to look again and more precisely at the socialism which I had embraced in order to build the social fabric to which the activities of the West London Mission were either committed or must contribute. Caring for old people, providing for homeless youngsters, setting up protection housing for recovered alcoholics, providing a home for delinquent girls, to say nothing of the pastoral responsibilities to all sorts of individuals in all sorts of needs, yield one indisputable corollary: we live in a class-ridden society where the idea of equality, whether in opportunity, condition, culture or life style, is a word without substance. It simply does not exist.

The people to whom those vegetables were delivered, were living in a different world both from the social workers who delivered the

94

goods and the ministers responsible for the problem which those vegetables had set. Socialism is the professed answer to the evils and inequalities of a class society. It begins in the assumption that such a divided society is morally wrong, that a united society is morally right, and that to move towards such a commonwealth is the priority of civilized behaviour. But how is that initial move to be made? Something has to be done immediately, and ninety per cent of social work, especially in church, is, as it were, the first aid to the victims while the ambulance is still on the way, and hospital recovery is a further stage away. Of course, even in a class-ridden society, the State offers a good deal of that first aid, yet, without socialism, there is no hospital to provide the final means of recovery. It is a bleak accusation of the society in which I have lived and tried to work, but the class divisions and inhumanities with which I was confronted in the thirties still exist today and, in some regards, are worse.

Moreover, if it be argued that some of the most objectionable elements in a class-ridden society have been modified by the welfare state and reduced by Labour governments, and that the climate they have introduced in its turn has softened attitudes among Conservative governments, socialism's priority is to change the system itself and not make it less objectionable. It is the foundation upon which our social life is reared and which is of paramount importance and demands attention.

Let no one imagine that this is a platitude. Coming up against 'the system' is the occupational frustration of the social worker but, as in so many other disagreeable elements in human experience, there is a tendency to turn a blind eye to the most obvious cause because to look at it would appear to be a useless waste of time and effort. Not so. The socialism I believe in begins in the practical increase of public power to change that system by Act of Parliament. We do possess workable democratic machinery, inhibited as it is by invested interest in an economic order which is capitalist. But the Parliament Act of 1910 which removed power from the House of Lords should encourage us to believe that parliamentary democracy in these islands is not under threat from military dictators and that, as Marx is reported to have written, a non-violent revolution could happen here.

There are, of course, those who insist that you cannot make people good by Act of Parliament. True, but you can make it much more difficult for them to be bad and, better still, you can so stimulate the good as to offer to ordinary people the satisfaction of behaving decently, and no one should underrate the results of such encouragement. At the same time, those who claim that Goodwill on Earth must largely begin in appropriate Acts of Parliament must obviously specify what sort of acts will help to usher in that socialist society, which takes the place of the class system that now prevails. If these Acts of Parliament and similar public measures are the means whereby a class society is to be replaced by a community, such programmes must be directed against the causes and occasions that produce such divisions. The answer is invariably an economic one. The irresponsible distribution of personal wealth; the inbuilt advantage, educationally, physically and culturally, of the privileged; the power of an establishment which is the residuary legatee of the property laws and inheritance its forefathers inaugurated; these are the principal causes of the class society – and the prating of those who proclaim the so-called truth that, if individuals can be saved from pride and greed, society will look after itself is little short of disgusting.

There is no need to be a Marxist to be convinced that changing the laws about property and possession and self-interest and the power of money can do more to unite society than a thousand appeals to the sinner to repent and mend his ways. Baptism by hosepipe is no alternative to legislation. On the other hand, government does not have to wait for the Kingdom of Heaven until a majority has become converted to its message. For, however swiftly personal conversion can move, political change can move much faster. Let me put it in terms of Clause Four in the creed of the Labour Party. This is the proposition that the means of production, distribution and control in the main requirement of life should be under public ownership or control. Such enactments as would move towards such a goal can safeguard that proposition long before its ultimate effects will appear and long before an electorate is fully converted to the basic principle it enshrines. The objection, by the way, that such an economic programme would debilitate enthusiasm and personal initiative has no foundation, although the Labour Party, while paying lip-service to this basic statement, has continued to give its support to the idea of a mixed economy. Such economies have no permanent place in socialist thinking, being inherently self-contradictory.

96

I prefer the evidence that fifty years of participation in the community of a Christian mission has brought into my experience – that only a socialist community can meet the true needs of individual people and the true purpose of social life. Such is my experience and I hold it now more strongly than ever, particularly when I endeavour to make sense of the world of the eighties.

CHAPTER ELEVEN

Twinkle, twinkle, little star,
Up in the sky so blue.
It's a jolly good job you are up so high
Or the boss would have had you too.

However improbable it may appear to the reader, this jingle immediately brings to my mind the House of Lords and, more importantly, it emphasizes in my experience a dominant feature of the society in which I have been living and working.

Alongside my responsibilities as Methodist minister in the West London Mission and my activities on Tower Hill, in 1965 I became involved in a third activity. I was invited by Harold Wilson to accept a life peerage, which I did. Although the offer came as a complete surprise to me, looking back on it I can see a number of reasons why perhaps Harold Wilson felt I might be of some use in the Lords. It was possibly because I was the Chairman of the Christian Socialist Movement at the time; or maybe the fact that I was rather more vocal than most other people equally devoted to the socialist cause. Certainly, there were others who could have fulfilled this opportunity at that moment.

In a number of respects this appointment had important effects upon my general pattern of activity. It provided me with a platform different from that in Hyde Park, and different of course from the pulpit. It was an opportunity and indeed a challenge. It is true to say that I found considerable difficulty in reconciling an acceptance of this offer with the socialist principles to which I was trying to commit myself, and I recognize that it does involve a compromise, but I would modestly argue that it is not a prohibitive one. While there is a second chamber, the House of Lords, it provides an opportunity for presentation of ideas and publicity for a programme which they otherwise would probably not receive.

Indeed, on matters such as pacifism and alcoholism, it has been my opportunity to raise or participate in debates in the House of Lords which has had considerable effect. I think it is not presumptuous to say that you can provide in three or four hours in the House of Lords the equivalent of a Royal Commission and have it reported the next day in Hansard. To some extent I think this is the value of a second chamber and, although I entirely disapprove of its hereditary constitution and of many of its legislative powers, I still believe that while it is there it can be used. I am, however, committed to its dissolution or at the very least such reform as will make it acceptable within the framework of democracy.

Now, to return to that opening jingle. Where did I first hear it? In this same House of Lords, which is not always the stuffy and formal institution many people imagine it to be. One afternoon, their lordships were debating a motion about property rights and I was sitting next to my friend, Lord Blyton – Bill to his acquaintances. A true Labour man, Bill appeared restive during the debate. Suddenly I heard an urgent whisper in my ear: 'Twinkle, twinkle, little star . . .' It was Lord Blyton reciting his version of the famous nursery rhyme. I am sure that, had J. K. Galbraith known of this jingle, he would have included it in his famous book, *The Acquisitive Society*, for it identifies a basic truth about the society in which we live. The ditty rings in my ears and evokes one of the most dominant lessons that I learned from talking and listening in the open air, as well as endeavouring to put the Gospel into practice as a Christian missioner.

Acquisitiveness is the enemy of the common good and it plays a disruptive part in every sphere of social living. Such is the verdict I have been forced to reach from the evidence of every kind of experiment in caring, whether it be in the realm of family welfare, financial insecurity, the rehabilitation of the alcoholic, or in the more private and personal area of honesty and moral seriousness. Yet hidden in the blanket condemnation of acquisitiveness, and it has a pejorative meaning for me as I use it, there is a false unity. There are two kinds of people who go to make up the acquisitive society and

99

they must not be confused in a general condemnation. In fact, their motives are almost entirely different.

The first is an old man, living alone. I visited him the other day and suggested that, while the weather was mild, could he not get out a bit, maybe come to one of the fellowship meetings at the church. He said that his outdoor shoes were worn out. He was saving up to buy a new pair. It was taking him a long time but in a month or two he reckoned it could be done and he would be out and about again. Strictly speaking, that old man was acquisitive. His intention was to possess a pair of shoes, and clearly there is nothing wrong in that. The effort to acquire the necessaries of life is itself a condemnation, not of those who have to make such an effort, but of the society in which they find themselves so bereft to start with. The acquisitiveness of the 'have nots' is fundamentally different in moral terms from that of the 'haves'. Unfortunately, it is often as practically disruptive. Quite apart from the almost inevitable resentment that such initial deprivation breeds, there is the more subtle reaction on the part of those who have never been in such need.

In general, they could not deny that the ambition of that old man to possess a pair of shoes is a just or even laudable one. They may, however, insist that self-help is the remedy rather than collective action by which his need will be met — as if the real responsibility lies with him and, if only he were more determined or more patient, he would not be in such a parlous situation.

I was brought up in a religious atmosphere where the non-conformist emphasis on personal responsibility led inevitably to the concept of the welfare state as no more than an emergency safety net, and it took some time for me to reach the kind of attitude of total rejection of this so-called non-conformist ethic, or at least the sense of its quite insufficient nature. Once again, it was the practical experience rather than the theory which changed my mind and altered my entire outlook.

I now find it nauseating in its hypocrisy, let alone its insensitivity. For the purpose of this comment on the prospects of social goodwill, the praiseworthy acquisitiveness of those who want to possess or to enjoy the amenities of a reasonable living standard is entirely right in itself, but at the same time it is an unavoidable cause of division and separation while the gap still widens between those who have and those who have not.

An assessment of the acquisitiveness of the other group – those who start off with what they need and proceed to covet what they want – leads me to a very different conclusion. They are, to my mind and experience, morally objectionable, deadly enemies of social justice. The causes or conditions that belong to the acquisitiveness of those who start off not from penury but from economic capability are not difficult to find.

It is all too easy to see how endemic is this acquisitiveness. I remember an occasion when, in the search for funds for one of our social requirements, we ran a bazaar and I persuaded an amiable, affluent lady to open the proceedings. When she did, she accompanied her remarks with an appeal to all of us to make sacrifices in the interests of the common good. As an illustration of what she meant, she announced that she herself had had to pension off two of her gardeners just recently.

Successful possessiveness leads both to power and to prestige. It feeds the desire to appear superior, it stimulates the wrong kind of *amour propre*, and it is the agent of pride, the worst of the seven deadly sins while, at the same time, it is an encouragement to commit the other sins as well. In short, it appeals to the lower elements in everybody. Over the centuries, this pride of possession has been curbed by the lack of opportunity to satisfy it, except among the privileged few. It has been further restricted because there were relatively few things to possess. Selfish satisfaction, for example, was a simpler quest because luxuries which are the means to that satisfaction were few and far between. Nowadays, opportunities for luxury are everywhere and an ever increasing assortment of material goods is made to whet the appetite and to attract the customer.

As Galbraith and others have pointed out, to acquire something so that it can serve a worthwhile purpose which is impossible to fulfil without it, may be praiseworthy and is certainly innocuous if there are enough of these things to go round. It is when the process becomes an end in itself that it is socially baleful. What is more, one of the chief pleasures of the acquisition is the advantage it bestows on the acquisitor because it puts him in a superior position to his fellow who is not as fortunate. So his interest will be to keep the product of his acquisitiveness in short supply because there is obviously no privilege with plenty.

Once again then, the prospect of Goodwill must be recognized as an unbreakable relationship between the individual and the social framework which is both the effect and the cause of human conduct. On the evidence, modern man is a mixture of selfishness and selflessness. The trouble is that the society he created while the selfishness was predominant (and this, by the way, is again the doctrine of original sin) continues to aid and abet that selfishness and to cripple the less selfish intentions which otherwise would take its place.

Nowhere is this fact more obvious than in the realm of advertising. As the available number of possible possessions multiplies, so that need to commend them increases. In the uncomplicated economy of an Elizabethan village, shall we say, the blacksmith had no need to advertise his horseshoes – the number of horses needing to be shod remained more or less stable and there was only one kind of horse's hoof. The modern phenomenon of the motor car responds to a completely different need. For one kind of horse as a means of locomotion and usefulness, there are a hundred different sorts of car. Moreover, the basic need of the blacksmith's shoe is sufficient to guarantee its sale. The modern car industry so multiplies the number of its shoes that the need factor in the sale of its product becomes quite insufficient.

Here surely is the justification for the moral condemnation of the acquisitive society as a menace to human goodwill and well-being. The market-place ceases to be where those who make the things that their fellows ought to use and enjoy are able to exchange their products with others engaged in the same creative activity. Instead, it becomes an arena in which the selfish interest of the producer encourages the sale of his product not for any concern for the common good or to satisfy a genuine need, but by the stimulation of motives and responses which have nothing to do with need but are a blatant appeal to far less justifiable elements in human nature.

So in the motor industry. For example, designers deliberately fashion car models to convey a 'phallic' image and so attract, consciously or unconsciously, the possible purchaser. Then what is called 'in-built obsolescence' is widely practised as a method of applying pressure on the consumer to purchase a new car and discourage the retention of the one that is less new. Make the car look out of date by quickly losing its polish or by changing the shape of the bonnet every twelve months and gullible car owners will be persuaded that, only if they buy the new model as soon as it appears in the show-rooms, will they be able to look the Joneses in the face.

In other areas of the acquisitive society, the level of truthfulness, let alone ethics, is lower still. There is a real difference between sitting at the wheel of your car and sitting at the bar of your pub. In the first instance, you may simply be going to work while in the second, you are almost certainly under the influence of a much less worthy motive. To acquire a glass of beer is basically self-indulgent, even if it is promoted as a form of fellowship, but such is the proliferation of such glasses of beer that the desire for it has to be buttressed with campaigns of propaganda of which the advertisements on the television screens are potent examples.

People, especially young people, are bombarded with a cannonade of assertions and claims that are inherently reckless when they are not completely false. Beer, we are told, is an essential form of nourishment if you are going to be healthy, popular and attractive. It is, of course, nothing of the sort. Alcohol may or may not have certain agreeable effects upon the person who drinks it, but he can get on perfectly well without it and, in the light of the drink problem with its catastrophic dimension today, he would be better without it.

As an unrepentant teetotaller, I regard advertisements for alcoholic drinks as one of the most disastrous aspects of the acquisitive society. In my experience, alcohol is incomparably the most dangerous of the social conditions in which modern society finds itself. It has been put to me thousands of times that my teetotalism is the result of training as a boy to regard alcohol as the devil in solution, and it is true that I was a member of the Band of Hope and that my father was a teetotal lecturer.

The effect of this upbringing is perhaps best exemplified by an episode which comes from my early days as a footballer. At school, we played on a football ground next to that occupied by a famous amateur team, 'the Casuals'. In one match in which I was playing at centre-half, I was badly concussed. I remember nothing of that day and did not wake up until early the following Sunday morning. What happened, therefore, was something of which I was not at the time conscious.

When it was discovered at half-time that I was concussed, it was suggested that I should be taken over to the trainer of the adjacent ground. He was most anxious to help and, having found out what was wrong with me, apparently said, 'I'll soon put him right – I'll give him a shot of whisky. That will do him a lot of good.' But, whereas before I had been more or less quiescent, at the mention of whisky I reacted most violently, despite my concussed state, and said on no account would I take any whisky and they had to substitute something of a less potent nature. When he later heard of the incident, my father was naturally delighted.

I am now completely satisfied that I have an unanswerable case in insisting that, whatever might be the place of light wines when the Kingdom of Heaven arrives, alcohol presents in our imperfect, dangerous and complicated society, a threat so great and so menacing as to require on the part of those who are endeavouring to be cooperators rather than individuals in that society, to go much further in a personal attitude of abstinence than would be required by a purely rational or particularly individualist principle of ethics.

From my experience of many years of participation in schemes for the reclamation of alcoholics, I have reached the conclusion that society cannot sustain the threat of alcohol, nor the increased violence, particularly among young people, that it causes. The increased availability of alcohol in cans and therefore at all times, has contributed to the sort of violence in the realm of sex which is not necessarily associated with blind drunkenness, but with a certain level of alcoholic intake.

If alcohol had appeared on the scene with the immediacy and the comparative suddenness with which heavy drugs such as cocaine and heroin have appeared, it would have been recognized by every sensible sociologist as presenting a far greater threat. We have come very largely to assimilate the concept of alcohol. This to me is no longer a valid way of endeavouring to baptize what may be in its social context one of the greatest evils with which we have to contend.

I would make two proposals for action in this area. Firstly, I believe that it would now be possible and entirely desirable to prohibit the advertisement of alcohol in any form. Secondly, there surely could and should be a very much more rigid control of the output and outlets. The beer can is almost a greater menace than any other form of incitement to, or provision for, the intake of alcohol at all hours and I would want to see it prohibited.

What, of course, is necessary at the moment is a campaign rather than a specific invitation to legal or constitutional action, and it is in that regard that I am writing here as an advocate believing that, when that advocacy has reached a certain stage, it will be much easier to see what are the political and social forms which such advocacy can assume.

Again, as an example of the capitalist system ignoring or rejecting all morality in principle and making up its own laws to serve its own interests, there could be no more convincing case than the cigarette. The close connection between smoking and lung cancer is, of course, proven, and the addiction to it has proved superior to any fear, however well grounded, of the consequences. For long enough, it has been accepted that the acquisition of that which gives pleasure or satisfaction, that is what we like, is an activity that is all too impervious to moral objections – it is hard enough to follow an educated conscience anyhow. But today, this flaw in our human make-up is exploited by spurious attempts to justify that acquisitiveness. Dress it up to look like a desirable way of getting the best out of life, exploiting all sorts of dubious elements of which, in other circumstances, we would be ashamed – greed, pride and snobbery, for example – in support of its objective. It is this compounding of a process, unacceptable in itself, which has demanded something more than appeals to truthfulness and ethical decency.

Advertising of cigarettes has been disciplined by Act of Parliament. A statement of truth must be appended to the propaganda – 'Cigarette smoking may seriously damage your health'. I would prefer that such moments of truth were expressed in the indicative rather than the subjunctive mood, and it is a pretty mild comment compared with the warnings of the medical profession. However, the principle behind this public intervention into the behaviour of the acquisitive society, is, I submit, the way forward to a less rapacious and more community-based society. Without such intervention, I cannot be persuaded that the real threat to social harmony can be met and then removed. What form would this intervention take?

The first and brute fact about any programme concerned with Goodwill is that a redistribution of wealth is the economic basis upon which all other projects must be built if they are to be effective. At the same time, legislation is necessary. For example, the vast advertising industry can be disciplined in relation to some of the products it stimulates, and absolutely prohibited in others.

105

To the extent that the acquisitive society is divisive and thoroughly undesirable in itself, the least of the requirements for abating its influence is to ease the pressure upon the susceptible would-be purchaser, so that his attention is not focused on accumulation as a worthy ambition for the full life. Where the so-called things that are accumulated are themselves undesirable or hurtful, they should not be advertised at all – indeed, I believe it should be a punishable offence to produce them in the first instance.

Having faced this issue as a daily problem in the social work of the West London Mission and as a moral question in open-air discussions, I am bound to accept that revolutionary political methods are the only ones which go deep enough and act effectively enough to turn our acquisitive social system into a cooperative commonwealth.

Now on the first page of any programme of action in this area, I would want to find the words which I originally accepted on the authority of the One who said them. I have now come to believe that they are completely correct in their own right. They are true because they correspond with reality:

> Lay not up for yourselves treasures on earth where moth and rust corrupt and where thieves break through and steal, but lay up for yourselves treasures in heaven where neither moth nor rust corrupt and where thieves do not break through nor steal, for where your treasure is there will your heart be also.

CHAPTER TWELVE

ONE OF JOHN Wesley's most quoted remarks is: 'The world is my parish'. And he expected his travelling preachers to adopt the same attitude to their own Methodist ministries. As one of them, I am aware now as I look back that only comparatively recently has the scope of that commitment to a world parish played a dominant role in my ministry and thinking.

My limited view of international questions and events dates back to the claustrophobia of the First World War in which I grew up. Then my formative years as a circuit minister were spent in the restrictive gloom that ushered in the Second World War, and in the exclusiveness which accompanied and followed it. One of the most devastating effects of international hostility is that it shrinks horizons and, not unnaturally, confines the areas of activity, both mental and practical, of those who live under its restrictions. Worse still, it pollutes all genuine knowledge of the world at large with the poisons of deceit and mutual suspicion. War shuts its participants and victims off from the real world.

It was not until after 1950 that I found the opportunity of true education about that world which indeed must be the parish of the would-be seeker of the Kingdom of God. In a number of evangelical excursions to the USA, Sri Lanka, East Germany, Poland, Australia and to the Far East, I was left in no doubt that many of my previous pronouncements on global matters, especially those made on Tower Hill, were, to say the least, impertinent. I simply did not know what I was talking about. When, in particular, I talked about the world community which was to be raised on the foundations of socialism, I did so from a standpoint of relative innocence as to what it was like to be living elsewhere than in London and in the British Isles.

I can recapture the new *Weltanschauung* most vividly in one particular experience when I was in Japan at the invitation of the Christian Churches (under the ecumenical umbrella provided by the State). Through an interpreter, I had the opportunity of preaching and of discussing social issues with a wide variety of audiences. As the Methodist chaplain to Pentonville from 1929 to 1936, I was particularly interested in the way that the penal system operated in Japan, and was glad to be able to visit a large prison in Kyushu. I was presented to about four hundred prisoners assembled in a large hall. They bowed, I bowed and, as we went through these formalities, I felt light years away from the block system of Pentonville. The strangeness intensified when the governor suggested that the prisoners might like to ask questions and I might be prepared to answer them. Incautiously I agreed.

The first question was: 'What is the gauge of the boiler of the latest British locomotive?' I had to confess that the answer defeated me. The second was: 'What do you think of the influence of Trotsky on the communist revolution in Russia?' Mercifully, I knew a little on that topic. But just as the prison itself was nothing like Pentonville, so in the pattern of the questions I was in a different world, years away from Hyde Park. Individually, many of the questions were remarkably familiar, but the background to them was totally different. By the end of the session, they had improved my knowledge of Zen but I doubt whether I had done much to acquaint them with the Christian Gospel, though I did my best to introduce it when we were not arguing about 'one hand clapping'. To put the cap on this extraordinary experience, I was told that many in that hall were already condemned to death. When I asked why they were still there, the answer was that the Home Secretary was a practising Buddhist and, so long as he was in office, the death sentence would not be carried out.

Not all my overseas contacts were as far out of my world as that one, but I can still remember so vividly, as I looked down from that platform in that hall at the faces of those prisoners and the grimaces they made which I took to be hostile but was assured were friendly, that the whole concept of Goodwill on Earth, held together in the tether of one great human community, took on a new and almost forbidding appearance.

Something of the same doubts and fears accompanied my efforts elsewhere. Speaking to a huge crowd on the Galle Face in Colombo, talking to Methodist groups in Poland and trying to understand their relationship with the Communist regime (and that was long before the emergence of Solidarity), endeavouring to persuade an American middle-west audience that I was a socialist but not therefore a communist (and getting nowhere) — all these various exposures to a world which was being reduced to the size of a neighbourhood, seemed increasingly to deny the possibility of that world ever attaining the quality of a neighbourhood.

As with the prospect of peace, so with the likelihood of goodwill: the wider the setting in which that future community is envisaged, the more formidable are the hindrances that are encountered. Nevertheless, I believe that to understand the problem of a world community, is not only to recognize what a colossal task it sets, but also to realize that the means of overcoming those difficulties may be found alongside. I am satisfied that they are discoverable in the context of episodes such as my visit to that Japanese prison. Once again, as in the domestic scene, it is much more profitable to look for answers in the political and economic sphere than to argue the case for a universal human being who would somehow unite all the divisive characteristics of particular human groups. Here, as in most other enquiries, the conviction I hold that man is basically the same creature wherever he happens to be, comes better from an examination of his particular day by day environment than as a general initial proposition about his essential nature.

Those prisoners in Kyushu were members of a nation state. In their case, one which represented in acute fashion elements that belong to such a social structure. For eight centuries before the Meigi reforms in the middle of the nineteenth century, Japan had been a group of walled cities related to one another but isolated from the rest of the world. Their political development had been towards one comprehensive walled city but such economic and political change had stopped at the coastline of Japan. When the country was 'opened up', as happened so quickly and dramatically, it found itself in a strange world but one in which the concept of the nation state was as deeply entrenched outside its own boundaries as it had been within them.

Now this is a rough and ready comment on a huge social phenomenon, but I would submit that a deeper investigation of this nation state confirms the contention that the enormous problems today in promoting Goodwill Among Men have much to do with the profound effect of the nation state on human behaviour. So to examine the characteristics of this form of human association is inseparable from any intelligent analysis of the future.

In quality as in quantity, the nation state is outstandingly violent and, in as much as that violence has been accepted as the chief weapon with which to further its aims, 'My country right or wrong' has generally been shortened to 'My country, right − ?' Furthermore, the nation state is inevitably predatory − cooperation for a common good to be shared by nation states together is swallowed up in the scramble for resources and possessions and the exploitation of the underdeveloped by the more powerful countries. I recognize that the more brutal aspects of colonialism have diminished, as much perhaps by the shrinkage of opportunity as by a change of heart, but in many instances the erstwhile colony or dependency has now simply become the satellite.

Nationalism remains the governing principle in the conduct of our human afffairs, and no one knows this better than the communist who, looking at the Soviet Union or China, must accept that Marx totally failed to see that nationalism would still prove stronger than any other political motivation.

There is, of course, one other element embedded in the theory and practice of the nation state − the fact that its administrative engine is capitalism, that is, a blend of selfishness and privatization. If the foregoing indictment of the nation state may appear too sweeping or harsh, it truly reflects my hatred of it. Although I try not to extend that hate to those who are its willing clients, I do not abate my conviction that its effects on us imperfect human beings stand obdurately in the way of human brotherhood.

If then the enactment of socialist measures to move towards the achievement of Clause Four is the augury of success in the domestic field in this quest for Goodwill on Earth, is there a parallel programme for a human society as a possible whole? The answer unfortunately is 'No', and for a simple reason. With all its faults, the nation state has one redeeming feature. It does provide for an overall authority and, if that authority is democratic at least in intention, then socialist legislation is a practical possibility. Internationally, no such unified authority exists. All states oppose a higher authority precisely because they are laws unto themselves.

No wonder that Lenin sought to overthrow the State as the necessary first stage to the introduction of what he called socialism, and believed that any remnants of the State which survived would 'wither away'. The State in the Soviet Union has not withered away, but the fault is not with socialism, but in the State capitalism of contemporary Russia.

As I see it, the beginning of an answer to the question, 'Is it possible to contemplate an harmonious family life for a human species which is divided by so much difference of outlook and behaviour?' must depend on the diminution of the causes that produce these divisions.

We are gregarious animals and take the imprint of the particular association which expresses that need to be together. Leaving alone then for the moment the question as to whether or not we have the ability to survive, hope for our future depends on the nature of the human grouping. We live in nation states and that grouping is bad. If we change it, we shall not have solved all our problems but will be in a far better position to do so. Moreover, we will be on the way to discovering what human beings can be and do when their social environment is less selfish and less violent.

I do not ignore the relevance of the immortal Bairnsfather cartoon from the trenches of the First World War: 'If you know of a better 'ole go to it', or, better still, the New Testament parable of turning the devil out of the house but not putting in a better tenant. The alternative to the nation state is some kind of world government — that is the 'better 'ole' for the incoming tenant. Only an administration that can command a global authority as obligatory as that which is possessed by individual nations, can face this challenge. A so-called United Nations, within which a security council provides for the maintenance of national autonomy when the interests of the great powers may be threatened, is no recipe for world government because it dodges the basic issue. By safeguarding the very powers of the nation state, it makes the wider authority largely inoperative.

Similarly, the European Economic Community which, it is claimed, is a step away from the nation state and towards a large loyalty, has not as yet shown evidence of even a federal authority among its members, let alone a merging of power into higher authorities than the parliaments of its members.

I agree that this transfer of power away from individual nations,

111

which actually exist, to a world government, which has never existed, is a vast step. Because of the thousand difficulties that thinking about it suggests, it is rarely considered by most people. Nonetheless if, as I have come to think, the Goodwill of a world community can only emerge in a society liberated from the shackles of the nation state, then world government must find itself upon the agenda of today's business. It is of no value as an ultimate aim as yet beyond the reach of those who cherish it. As Lenin observed, revolutions (and this would be the ultimate revolution) can only be successfully undertaken when the proletariat have reached a certain level of understanding of both the necessity for, and the inevitable success of, their cause.

That preparedness is certainly not evident when it concerns a world government operating a socialist programme. The hope of Goodwill lies in a classless society serving the commonwealth. The hope of approaching that sort of community lies first and above all in the abolition of the principal social system which stands in the way, that is the nation state. To turn that hope into faith waits upon a genuine understanding of the problem, linked with a profound sense of commitment to its solution.

We have much to do and the hour is already late. Some of the machinery of world government exists in the United Nations already, but the spirit of world government has yet to be generated.

The family. Taken in 1952, this photograph shows my wife Marie with, on her left, Caroline and Ann and, on her right, Bridget and Judy

Speaking at Westminster Cathedral in 1978

Speakers' Corner, 1983

(Methodist Record

Preaching at St Mary-le-Bow, Cheapside

Cutting the cake with Marie and Michael Foot on my 80th birthday

CHAPTER THIRTEEN

THE MEETING ON Tower Hill was particularly rowdy and some of the heckling decidedly hostile when I became aware of a policeman standing immediately in front of me. He made himself known. I was to get down. When I asked him why, he said that I was committing an offence. Since I had been speaking there for over fifty years without, as far as I knew, contravening the law, I naturally found this difficult to understand. So I asked him what offence he had in mind.

'You are causing an obstruction,' he replied. This seemed preposterous enough in itself but the punchline came when I asked what I was obstructing.

'You are obstructing the Tower of London,' he said.

I later learnt that the police were acting on a tip-off that terrorists were planning a bomb attack on the Tower but, even if I had known the background, I would have refused to abandon the meeting for I was causing no obstruction whatever. The policeman hauled me down from the platform, arrested me and told me to wait for the wagon. But instead of the wagon, a senior officer soon arrived. He quickly admitted that a mistake had been made and told me I was free to continue the meeting. I said that I hoped the constable would not be penalized for the mistake and received the answer: 'He will not be penalized, but he will be informed.'

That episode, although trivial in itself, contained one element that is far from trivial. I mentioned that it was a meeting in which there was a great deal of hostile opposition rather than amicable discussion, and a casual visitor might well have imagined that there was little love lost in the rowdy encounter. Yet the moment I was threatened with the law, unfairly as it appeared to the crowd, they were all on my side – communists, atheists, regular hecklers, the lot. Whenever I think of that Wednesday, I find a refreshment of spirit and a revived optimism about the quest for Goodwill Among Men, and my account, while providing ample evidence of the profound difficulties that stand in the way of its realization, would be radically incomplete unless it included also the deep and abiding impression of hopefulness evoked by that incident.

I have argued so far that this innate disposition towards the good rather than the bad needs to be scaffolded politically and economically in the first instance, if the building behind that scaffolding is to stand up. Nevertheless, to complete the picture, or finish the story as it were, I should consider how this innate tendency towards the good can be so channelled and stimulated as to turn the hopefulness which it engenders, into faith and conviction.

The justification that I have come to accept for the socialist creed in general and the Labour Party in these islands, lies in the relationship of a political party to this basic principle which, given the right opportunity or stimulus, can turn that political party into a crusade. The Labour Party has become the appropriate vehicle, in the foreseeable future, for that blend of practical social measures, and of the natural impulse towards good which can imbue and safeguard them. This is not to say that the Party is already socialist – it is far from it – but it is the one political soil in which the seeds of socialism, already there, can grow and flourish.

Looking back, I would think that the Labour Party over which Attlee presided probably came nearer to the concept of socialism as I sought to believe in it than on reflection did the governments under Wilson and Callaghan, where the impending storms of debate and difficulty within the Party were already mounting. The contemporary issues as between what are loosely called the right and the left, or the militant right and the militant left, give me cause for very considerable perturbation as to whether in the past I have looked upon the Labour Party rather too easily as the totally appropriate vehicle for the expression of what I and many others have to believe is the socialist creed. What I would reinforce is that only in a resolution of present difficulties based on a more radical socialism, will the party be finally united. The only way left is the only way right.

Although a Labour Party working within the framework of this

114

nation state is inevitably a flawed political instrument, it is not totally inhibited, as a Tory Party must be, in the struggle to move towards world government. Notwithstanding the gap that still yawns between the Labour Party existentially and the Labour Party ideally, I remain committed to it. I make no apology for concluding these reflections on the proximate chances of social harmony with a general view of the moral and instrumental theory of socialism that can hold the party together.

What is the philosophy of politics that absorbs and expresses in one comprehensive idea the variety of the rational, emotional and wilful ingredients of social life? If it is not a Marxian determinism, nor a utilitarian solution (and neither of these ideologies appears to me to be supportable), then what is it? I am satisfied that it is necessary to go beyond philosophy to find out. The question is a theological one and the answer depends on the third part of the heavenly declaration to which I will come in the final chapters of this book. What I will consider here is 'applied theology' that is, the application of 'pure' theology as I find it in the Sermon on the Mount. Here is, for me, the complete picture which brings together and unites the various questions concerning Goodwill on Earth to which I have addressed myself.

This statement by Jesus, whether recorded as one sermon or a digest of many, has enabled me to make sense of apparently conflicting experiences of success and failure in promoting Goodwill, to say nothing of the equally conflicting experiences in political activities. This sermon in the New Testament is delivered in the language of the family. The vocabulary is that which is used to describe family matters. The conclusions that are drawn are those which follow the acceptance of the family pattern as intrinsic to an understanding of what is right and what is wrong. In short, the concept of the family is the foundation for real thinking and good living.

So the Kingdom of God, or the idea of Goodwill Among Men, is the extension of the principles of the individual family to cover the entire mix of human relationships. This is simply and explicitly set out in the family prayer which starts with the invocation to Our Father and immediately requires us to think of ourselves as brothers and sisters. Daily bread is necessary and is a fatherly responsibility, but it is for us, rather than for me, that I am instructed to ask for it.

My relationship to others is governed by the fact that we both have the same kind of problems, because we belong to the same household and need to forgive our fellow members, as we would wish them to forgive us. I will quote some of the dominant statements about the way in which this family background requires particular responses to particular needs. I do so rather than simply refer to what is written as if the reader is well acquainted with the text. There is to me astounding ignorance of the document as a whole, both inside and outside congregations. Snippets from it are familiar to people who go to church but, from my experience, I am bound to wonder how many, even of those who would call themselves Christian, know this sermon as a whole and have read it at one sitting in its entirety beginning with the words, 'And seeing the multitudes' (in Matthew's Gospel, chapter V, verse 1) and only stopping at the concluding words, 'And not as the scribes' (Matthew VII, 29).

Our human needs are to be met in the family spirit and not on the basis of merit or moral worthiness. 'Consider the lilies of the field, they toil not neither do they spin'. On the basis of the work ethic they are a lazy bunch, 'yet Solomon in all his glory is not arrayed like one of these' purple wild flowers. 'Consider the fowls of the air' – they have no sense of economic responsibility – 'they do not gather into barns and yet your heavenly father feeds them'. 'And if God so clothes the grass of the field which today is and tomorrow is cast into the oven shall he not much more clothe you' – and on the same basis of need not merit. 'Your heavenly father causes his sun to shine on the evil and good and his rain to fall on the just and the unjust' – the bad man is not condemned to live in the dark and rain does not only water the good man's garden. We are to imitate his providence in our own behaviour. In this family relationship both your neighbour and your enemy belong together, however much they may abuse that fellowship. You shall 'love your neighbour as yourself', and what is much more, you shall love your enemy because he is still a member of the family. 'Do good to those who hate you and despitefully use you' – that is, regard them as brothers or sisters even when they try to break the family spirit. And here comes the otherwise inexplicable evidence that this moral ideal is in fact practicable. The Sermon on the Mount declares what is already there, though frustrated and unrecognized: 'What man of you if his son ask bread will give him a stone or if he ask a fish will give him a serpent'; and 'if ye then being evil know how to give good gifts to

116

your children, how much more will your heavenly father give good gifts to them that ask him'. So, if you carry out that practice in the Kingdom of God, then what you seek you are sure to find. The Kingdom is at hand and your business is to put it in hand. The family spirit works, it is existential – it is true realism. There is an illustration of this realism in an aspect of this teaching which at first blush may appear surprising, almost dangerous. It is to be found in Luke XI, 5–8, but I will presume to put it in my own words.

A neighbour wakes a man up in the middle of the night. Unexpected visitors have turned up at his house and he has run out of bread. Can he borrow a loaf? While the man may not respond and give him the loaf out of sympathy for his neighbour's plight, he will say to himself, 'Though I'm not going to help him because he is my neighbour, if I don't answer he'll go on knocking, the baby will wake up and nobody will get any more sleep. So I will give him the loaf if only to get rid of him and save myself further trouble'. Neighbourliness, like honesty, is the best policy. It works in practice even when its finer spirit is absent.

Here, in this sermon from long ago, is the root principle of socialism. The family life around the family table, the sharing both of the responsibility and of the things needful for the family life and welfare of all as the aim of each of its members. But what gives a kind of bonus is the realization that, in certain circumstances, we already accept some of its conditions and practise some of its precepts.

For example, the food on most family tables is not only available for those who can pay for it, nor does someone beat the dinner gong to start a scramble for the food and the devil take the hindmost. The food in Pentonville is adequate if not appetizing, the clothing covers the right surfaces and the roof does not leak. Until the advent of the welfare state, a prison came nearer to family life than many a slum outside its gates – and I have worked in both.

The governing injunction in this body of teaching is that to 'seek first' this kind of universalized family life is the priority because not only does it come first as bread, the most immediate and demanding of our needs, but also it is the 'bell-wether' of everything else that is is worthwhile looking for. All other desirables will be added. That is the thesis of socialism for me and the objective of the politics and economics which can prove the way for its benefactions. As I see it, Clause Four is the natural consequence in public terms, not of some supposed determinism discoverable from an analysis of economics, but of an understanding of the nature and meaning of the human family and an application of the findings of that inquiry.

The elimination of the class society is the product of the acceptance by everyone as belonging to that family, whether knocking at the door as a visitor or even trying to break it down as an enemy. The welfare state must be inclusive if it is to be genuine. Equality before the law is the outcome of universality of status. The right to enjoy the food at that family table is determined by a relationship in which a common need is paramount and the only privilege is to 'pass the salt' not to appropriate it.

If, however, I were to bring these observations to an end at this point as if they were either self-evident or conclusive, I would be guilty of avoiding two problems. Firstly, to propound the doctrine of the family as the source of authority for a world political and economic creed, can only take off, as it were, if those to whom it is advocated know what the advocates are talking about. The vocabulary must be commonly intelligible. Now for me, like many others, this has always been straightforward. Father, mother, brother, sister, family table, family prayers, family responsibilities, are all words which ring the same bell which is sounded in the Sermon on the Mount, and even the words about loving enemies because they are still members of the family, though going much further, are nevertheless further along a familiar road.

It is an almost entirely different situation when these words conjure up no such sense of fellowship or love or cooperation or personal confirmation. I think of my time as chairman of Mayford Approved School for delinquent boys from 1960 to 1964. In so many cases when the boys were from broken homes, a socialism expressed in family terms made not the slightest impression upon them. We were speaking a foreign language. Father was the man who left home for another woman. Brother was the elder boy who had taken the first opportunity of going off on his own. The family table meant little better than a free-for-all and, in many cases, there was not enough food on it anyhow. The very word 'home' was a sick joke. To expect a welcome response to the advocacy of family life as the pattern and pledge of Goodwill Among Men demands an acquaintance with its basic characteristics as an absolute priority. If, therefore, that acquaintance cannot begin in the direct experience of those to whom it is prescribed, its credibility must be elsewhere – in the realm of public administration.

118

Once again, the pietistic or individualistic insistence that the first step towards social well-being is in a personal change of heart and attitude contradicts my increasing experience. Political action is the grammar book of social change for the better, and is indispensable if the language of that social change is to be intelligible, let alone constructive. Acts of Parliament which seek to do away with social injustice can at the same time familiarize the community as a whole with the kind of public behaviour that can take its place. Such is their vocation as well as their duty. For example, to lift something of the burden that bears upon the old, to care for them by enacting measures which remove the economic strains that they can no longer absorb, is a civilizing public duty. But it is also more than that. It is a reminder of the sort of family relationship which I believe is already half-acknowledged. In the Proustian sense, it enlivens or recalls a concept of the good life. It educates as well as enacts. Those who cannot read the meaning of Goodwill because the language is a foreign tongue as far as their experience goes, can find it translated, at least in fact, in the welfare state so that they can read, learn and inwardly digest it there.

Yet the word 'family' conveys different meanings to different human groups — and here is the second problem. A family in this context calls up for a Moslem an image initially different from that which it stimulates in the mind of, shall we say, a Victorian parent or the leader of an Israeli kibbutz. Missionaries seeking to spread the Gospel in areas of Africa, where polygamy appears as an indispensable foundation for a stable family life, necessarily find much of the Sermon on the Mount, which assumes monogamy, extremely difficult to advocate and in some respects impossible to apply.

I have come to believe that a real distinction must be drawn between fundamental laws that are to be found in every kind of gregariousness which claims to be a family relationship, and particular expressions of those laws which may apply to different stages in social development and differing cultures. There is a real difference between Western customs in the family group, and universal principles that belong to all relationships worthy of that description. To put family behaviour patterns accurately into either the category of variable custom or that of its basic nature, is an almost forbidding task. Are patriarchal or matriarchal societies the result of custom? Does the women's movement represent demand for, or the existence of, a fundamental relationship between father

119

and mother hitherto unrecognized and unpractised and into what category, if any, should a universal form of marriage be put?

In the present discussion, there are three propositions which, though not solving these social conundrums, can provide the wages of going on in the right direction.

The first is to recognize the principle of family life which is common to all examples of it. The family is a social unit, not a casual association of individuals. The second is the sharing of the means of life required for each member. Proceed upon the common practice of giving the members in the first instance what they need, and only thereafter expecting the contribution to the entire family which can be rendered by those so satisfied. Finally, believe that the answers to the other problems that now appear insoluble cannot at present be found precisely because, until now, all family groupings have operated within a more or less hostile ecclesiastical or economic climate. Begin to provide that more universal economic climate and the varieties or social cohesion will tend to wither away where they separate differing family groups, leaving the family life of the Sermon on the Mount and the Kingdom of Heaven as the 'master key' to unlock all the doors to Goodwill Among Men.

This is my belief but I do not forget that such a confidence relies on whether or not the family life is an achievable objective and that, in its turn, depends on the credibility of the third proclamation made by the Heavenly Host: 'Glory to God in the Highest'. If God is there to be glorified, then Goodwill is there to be realized.

But is He?

Part Three

Glory to God

CHAPTER FOURTEEN

THE CHRISTIAN RELIGION has been called the 'Drama of Eternal Redemption' played out on the human stage, and I find this a welcome change from some of the more metaphysical ways of thinking about it. For if the song of the Heavenly Host at the first Christmas can be regarded as the prologue to that drama presented on its opening night, I am satisfied that the order in which the three statements were made is no coincidence. Peace on Earth and Goodwill Among Men are not simply to be added to Glory to God as making up a triumvirate of future delights in the unfolding drama. Every indication of what follows this prologue shows that Glory to God is the prerequisite condition upon which the others absolutely depend. To give Glory to God, to acknowledge His existence, to appreciate His benevolence, and to gear human hopes in humble obedience to His will, each is the foundation upon which to build the future, and there is no other foundation upon which such a happy prospect for tomorrow can be built.

It may be argued that any attempt to treat this prologue should begin at the right place with Glory to God, and not with its consequences, for is not the attempt in these pages to consider Peace and Goodwill first likely to convey the impression that Glory to God is somewhat of an afterthought? Certainly not. I would claim that there is a sufficient reason for the order in which Glory to God, though of supreme significance as I believe it is, be treated after the consideration of the other two and not before them.

Perhaps the most valuable precept that my Cambridge philosophy tutor, the great Dr F. R. Tennant, left upon my mind was that the 'inductive' process of reasoning should, wherever possible, be preferred to the 'deductive' one. Deductiveness is that process of thought which begins with the conclusion to be arrived at and thereafter the evidence is produced so as to confirm that conclusion: God exists, and our intellectual business is to find the evidence which fits that initial statement. The student of philosophy will know that, until Francis Bacon's repudiation of it, this was the accepted method used by most Christian scholars.

Inductiveness, on the other hand, postpones the conclusion and makes it dependent upon the evidence, all of which must be acceptable in so far as it is either factual or the outcome of the examination of hypothetical conclusions. For those who follow this path, the existence and nature of God is not an arbitrary assumption protected by a selective process of confirmatory evidence but is the outcome of an enquiry. Its existence and nature constitute the reasonable verdict of the trial between truth and error, a verdict that is only credible because it is the 'summing up' and never comes before that stage has been reached. For that reason, I have reserved consideration of the message which was the first in the order of deliverance, and will now try to substantiate it as the acceptable conclusion of the evidence that has been marshalled in respect of Peace on Earth and Goodwill Among Men.

What then of this tremendous phrase, 'Glory to God', has been illuminated or at least present in my own experience? The various episodes which I will use here do two things for me. They make sense of the argument for a Christian faith and, at the same time, they turn the hesitations and doubts and even apparent contradictions about Peace and Goodwill into the belief that all things work together for good to them that love God.

The greatest question of all, as to whether there is a God, never crossed my infant mind. I may have been singularly immature as a senior schoolboy. I would only plead that the reality of my Christian home life made the acceptance of the basic beliefs of theology unquestionable so long as I lived under its protection. My memory of those days is that what discussions took place about Christianity and what problems those discussions either reflected or raised, were almost entirely within the moral rather than in the theological area.

I cannot remember ever discussing with my parents or ever hearing them discuss matters of theological debate as between various Churches for example. What I do recall is the over-arching sense of moral responsibility which that Christian faith engendered

124

and demanded, and those issues that were raised were in most cases issues of behaviour in which I was invariably the delinquent and for which I was either taken to task or was involved in improving lectures from my parents. All this was acceptable to me mainly because it was so important to them. It was the complete sense of sincerity with which things were presented rather than as matters they were required to believe or to insist upon. They carried conviction.

Some of the rules which I was commended to keep no longer seem binding, and in some cases are undesirable. I was enjoined, in the strict Sabbatarian climate of my home and Church, to practise on Sunday a code of behaviour which included repeated attendance at church, the reading of suitably edifying books like *Eric, or Little by Little* and going to bed early on Sunday which had more to do with the exhaustion from our Sunday observances than any spiritual motives. Moreover, on the negative side, I had to resist the intake of alcohol as 'the devil in solution'. I had to stand resolutely against any activity which could be called gambling, and to resist any invitation to the dance – though I remember that rhythmic exercises were permitted, and it is remarkable what we were able to get in under that category.

That Christian home life from the age of about eleven to fifteen was very largely lived within the restrictive framework of the First World War, and in those war days the practising of the Christian faith was completely absorbed within the framework of doing one's duty, going to church with great regularity and looking forward to a world in which things would be better. I cannot remember any moment of intellectual rebellion, although I can remember to my discredit the occasions of moral rebellion and their traumatic consequences. I think it must be added that, whereas my mother was of a very inquiring mind, her preoccupation – as headmistress of a school – was far more with what I ought to be doing and what I ought not to be doing, than with what I ought to be believing. My father, on the other hand, had practically no intellectual difficulties as far as I can remember. His was a straightforward up-and-down belief that he was under God's protection and love and must take care not to be under God's judgment as well.

My parents made considerable sacrifices in order to enable me to go to Cambridge and, although my father insisted on my rendering an account of my spending of his money every week and took very direct action if I failed to let him know what it was, I have a recollection of profound gratitude for the way in which they resisted the inclination to try and fit me into their mould. They were most charitable in the way in which they tolerated, if not agreed with, my increasing intellectual difficulties to say nothing of my pacifism and the beginnings of my social conscience.

The difficulties had started in earnest when I went up to Cambridge and, as I relate what almost immediately happened to me, I can recollect the shock as if it hit me only yesterday. After I had visited my tutor to find out what I had to do during the week, I went to see the local Methodist Sunday School Superintendent as to my Sunday activities. This may sound most peculiar but for me at that stage it was entirely natural, as was my acceptance of his request that I should take a junior Sunday School class. I was to read for a History Tripos, and a fellow undergraduate, as it turned out a friend in disguise – and a very good disguise at the time – gave me Bury's *History of Rationalism* to read. I read it with increasing horror and found myself an atheist even before I had finished it. I know now that such a document need not disturb a more mature theism but I was in no position to counter its implications. I was totally unprepared and defenceless in the face of the attack. I felt that, in honour bound, I ought to tell the Sunday School Superintendent that as an atheist I could not very well start to teach Christianity in a Sunday School class and he saw the point at once.

But if for him the incident might have been closed, it was not for me. I had no intention of abandoning the fellowship of the Church merely because I felt no longer able to subscribe to its creed. The Church was my second home. That Sunday School Superintendent was a wise man. He wondered whether, despite my atheism, I would still think it honourable to play the piano for the hymns even if I could not subscribe to the words. I leapt at the offer and so, throughout the period of my atheism, I continued as Sunday School pianist.

As I recall it, that experience epitomized two of the prime factors about a religious belief or the absence of it. They are both cardinal for any effective approach to an optimistic outlook. Belief in God is an intellectual and moral adventure. It is not a forgone conclusion. I regained my faith, a rather different one from that which the *History of Rationalism* so devastated, not by the repudiation of the objections to it as if they were not only worthless but impious, but by slow and often painful process of accepting many of these objections, and yet finding reasons for regarding them as insufficient to undermine the basic concepts of a Christian belief.

Perhaps an incident on Tower Hill is apposite here. A young man came to see me in great distress. He and his wife had been married for only a few months when she contracted a fatal illness and died. He had listened from time to time to what I had to say about the love of God. How did I reconcile that love with his sorrow? He could not believe in a God of love in the face of his bereavement. I prattled about the philosophic relationship between the problem of evil and original sin, and a future life when all would be revealed and so on. It left him comfortless and I heard nothing more of him until one day he wrote to me from Australia where he had made a new and happy life. In the letter he wrote:

> I got my faith back when I stopped thinking that I had to choose between the arguments for believing and the arguments for not believing. It was when I came to see that I was free to make up my mind, rather than letting the arguments make it up for me. I found that neither those on one side nor those on the other could convince me. I had to choose. I did so and I know what it is now to live by faith.

He found the key to a genuine religious experience and that is what happened to me in my first year at Cambridge. There is no knock-down proof of the existence of God which can stun us into acceptance and at the same time anaesthetize us against any contrary arguments. I have found over and over again that the problem of pain presents almost as sound arguments for disbelieving in the love of God as those which can be mustered to support it. Similarly, in the quest for Peace and Goodwill, the humanist explanation of their non-appearance as yet, and the rationalist rejection of some divine purpose behind the flux of events, are not easy to counter with a world-embracing faith. I have come away from Hyde Park many times leaving the questioner still in charge of his arguments and with the theological answer to his questions very much still in contention.

The faith to which I returned after a period of months as an atheist was a pilgrimage of trust and much of it has been hard going. To use a phrase that is colloquial but basically true, Christianity for

127

me became the gamble of betting my life on Christ. It has increasingly come to mean a life insurance policy rather than a wager, and what was once a gamble appears more and more like a certainty. This is both the exercise and the justification of the inductive approach to a belief in God and the glory He merits. Start with the evidence, and not a preferential selection of it. Such evidence will not of itself add up to a conclusive proof one way or the other. Then exercise your freedom to assemble that evidence in patterns, as the modern exponents of the induction process insist and, as you try out those 'experiments in synthesis', you arrive at general conclusions that work and others that do not.

The experimental use of the evidence that I was so dramatically compelled to recognize in my first year at Cambridge confirmed for me a theistic stance which works as nothing else does. Despite innumerable failures to live up to that commitment, I find that to interpret, or try to interpret, the issues that require a reasonable answer in the light of the Christian Gospel, does begin at the right place and does lead to the right answers. Whatever the problem, to face it from the standpoint of God's good news becomes the realistic as well as the optimistic approach. I saw a placard the other day which announced: 'Jesus can answer all your doubts'. Whether the sponsor of that placard was aware of the complex background to that claim I do not know, but I am nevertheless humbly sure he is right.

The other element in my first and decisive encounter with the credibility of the Christian promise is not primarily a matter of belief or doubt but it has had an equally dramatic effect. My reaction to Christianity as a creed was temporarily transformed, but my reaction to Christianity as a way of life remained largely unaffected. Naturally, prayers were out if I believed God was not there to hear them. Equally naturally, reading the Bible and attending sermons lost their particular importance if they were nothing better than fictional. But Christianity as a way of life was very much more than these devotional practices. It has been said that religion is 'what a man does with his loneliness'. My reaction to the fellowship of the Church which accompanied my loss of faith or its doctrines was a dramatic awareness of this faith. I am grateful that it happened so early in developing my self-consciousness and its significance has grown with the years.

At the same time I am aware of the objections that can be raised against treating this reaction with a seriousness it does not deserve.

It can be argued that a churchmanship which is an extension of a happy domestic life is attractive for all sorts of reasons and is not invalidated because some of them no longer apply. Church for me was where I made my friends and I kept their friendship in good repair by regular contact. It was where I spent much of my leisure time, singing in choirs and taking part in dramatic adventures and pageants. In short, I was at home and at school in the local Methodist church and I belonged there. Although it would be foolish to deny that such facts had a great deal to do with my new-found intention to cling to the Church when its claims had been torn from my grasp, they will not do as a sufficient explanation. That the Church satisfied for me certain fundamental needs, other than the need to find an intellectual basis for my life, demands a reason or reasons that cannot be shrugged off as obvious, and therefore insignificant.

Looking back, I am sure that my imperative desire to stay within the fellowship of the Church and the satisfactions that I found there, represented a reality about religion just as basic as my desire to confide in its teaching. We are bidden to love God with heart and mind. The inability fully to obey that invitation with the mind does not prevent the obedience of the heart. This, I recognize, is a dangerous statement to make and one which is easy to misunderstand and consequently to reject. Nevertheless, it happened to me and so it radically affects the relationship of this religious involvement with the prospects of Peace and Goodwill.

This episode in my spiritual pilgrimage is an example of how unwise it is to imagine that the reality of a religious experience can only enter through one door and that is the door of the intellect. Naturally, those who do pass through that door are more articulate because the instruments they use are words – you cannot profess a creed without words. Yet we all know that the reality of love, for instance, does not depend on articulation – in many cases words get in the way rather than point to it. The fellowship of a Church can make the love of God real for those who share its life and gather at the table of its Lord, and it is a gratuitous insult to claim that they are the victims either of a pipe-dream or a conspiracy.

I wanted to stay in the Church for I had no desire to leave that spiritual hearthfire and try for bed and breakfast in coldly academic lodgings. Once again, I return to Pascal's reminder of the 'reasons of the heart', which can be as valid and convincing as those which are usually associated with the mind. Man is made by God for God and is therefore restless until he rests in Him. That alone explains the comfort and assurance he experiences when he partakes of the fellowship of those who look to God and give him glory. He finds himself at home. In the second place, man is not made up only of thoughts and feelings. It requires no psychological profundity to recognize volition as the other ingredient of our make-up alongside thought and feeling – we are willing creatures as well as contemplative and sensitive ones. What we *do* must have a dynamic effect on what we are or what we become. This I have found to be the other lesson which I began to learn during my atheistic spell, and though I was not cognisant of it at the time, it was put in a nutshell by none other than one of the Moravian pastors who advised John Wesley, when he was passing through a time of theological doubt: 'Preach faith until you get it.'

The injunction to the clergy to 'practise what you preach' is enthusiastically and regularly proposed to me on Tower Hill and I have no doubt that such is a necessary warning, but how many of those who insist on such a requirement of the preacher are seized of Martin Buber's injunction to practise in preaching a faith which only becomes real as the result of such action? The exercise of the will is also an experience of the real world. That same fellowship in the Church which gave me the satisfaction of feeling at home also gave me the house rules of that home. It was in the spirit of obedience to the rules that the reality of the family life of the Church validated itself. The practice came first, long before I understood the sort of living that was to be the outcome of that practice.

I have mentioned the Christian code of behaviour that was so much part of my family life. Some of that code I now regard as misguided, yet much has remained with me. I still remain a teetotaller on the social grounds which I have explained rather than the more personal attitude to alcohol as in itself an inadvisable indulgence. I do not gamble and, without being a moral snob, I fail to see how those who take the Kingdom of God seriously and embrace socialism as the political machinery with which to inaugurate it, can justify such a selfish distribution of wealth. I have danced – taking into account the words of that great Methodist, Dr Maltby, who when challenged with the question, 'Can Christians dance?' replied, 'Some can and some can't.'

Over the years I have found it right to alter some of these laws, to reject others, and to add to their number: to practise as far as I am free to do, the law of pacifism; to change some of the patterns of the churchmanship of my youth, away from its Sabbatarianism to a more even spread of worship (and particularly eucharistic worship) over the seven days of the weeks, to obey the challenge of the modern society in which I am involved and often incriminated, and to practise politics as diligently as I was once called upon to practise holiness.

However, what is important is not the question as to what particular moral laws demand practise, but the principle that lies behind the recognition of the difference between what is right and should be obeyed and what is wrong and should be refused. I believe that, just as there are reasons from the heart for the reality of God, so there are reasons from the will which are equally persuasive. Once we recognize that we ought to do good and we ought not to do evil, and that individual actions which we take in this field do not invalidate this principle, even if they are themselves based on wrong judgments or moral values, we are entitled to believe that such a moral foundation which ought to be built upon is an authentic presumption that only God could have put it there; this is the pragmatism that justifies belief.

Kant put it infinitely better than I have been able to do with what he calls the 'categorical imperative'. I followed that requirement when I determined to stay in the Church until I found a faith. That experience confirmed the scripture which says: 'He that doeth the will shall know of the gospel.'

There are two final comments which should be added to the general questions which this traumatic episode raised for me. First, although the Sunday School at Cambridge did not provide me with the arguments and reasons which later on renewed my faith, it did keep me within an environment which increasingly confronted me with the reasons of the heart and will which were so real and central to the religious life which made up that fellowship of believers. Christianity, after all, is a way of life itself and I was mercifully saved from the monumental mistake of separating myself from that way of life just because one aspect of it − and unquestionably a very important one − was obscured. This, I believe, is the claim that appears so impertinent when it is arrogantly asserted that there is 'no salvation outside the church'. Whatever narrow and totalitarian meaning has been attached to this statement, when it is intended to

131

mean that there is no salvation that can fully exist outside the Christian society, I can vouch for it.

The second comment has to do with the particular consequence that attends a condition of non-belief when it is lived in an environment without those elements of heart and will which, in a fellowship of people who do believe, provide convincing evidence that such belief is credible. In such a condition of alienation from religion as a way of living, is it not possible that the distinction between right and wrong may itself disappear or not appear at all? It can, and indeed it does if I have not drawn a false conclusion from an experience I had while Chairman of Mayford Approved School.

It was my responsibility with others to interview boys there whose term of residence was running out, and to decide whether or not they were fit for release. At some of these interviews with boys from broken homes or from no background that could possibly be described in homely language, there seemed no way whatever of appealing to their better nature – they appeared totally unresponsive to ethical terms like 'better' or 'worse', 'good' or 'bad'. The moral dimension simply was not there, or was certainly so dormant as to be of no conscious significance.

Now everything in my own experience almost automatically rejects such a condition, but there seems to be increasing evidence in our modern secular society, unprecedented in so many of its characteristics, that such a hypothesis is the only one which can account for some at least of the more horrific crimes, and the otherwise inexplicable prevalence of violent, mindless, and anti-social behaviour. Is it too much to claim that religion, and that means some kind of Church, is the custodian of this ethical dimension, that it is not necessarily inborn and that, if the absolute difference between right and wrong as standards of behaviour is not demonstrated there, they may not come to life at all? I am still not sure and I almost automatically react against what could be regarded as a doctrine of 'total depravity'.

Yet for me, and for those who indignantly repudiate this equation, it must be true that our future well-being is a meaningless phrase unless men and women come to know the difference between selfishness and sacrifice, craftsmanship and craftiness, love and desire, while at the same time accepting the responsibility of a practical choice between them.

It is not enough to assert the dogma of God's existence and nature in order to safeguard His Kingdom. For all practical purposes, God is only there when He is seen to be there. 'God walks in the garden of His church where men have ceased to walk, let alone to listen. No wonder they do not meet Him.'

No wonder that they do not even hear him speak.

CHAPTER FIFTEEN

THE FIRST TIME I heard someone declare 'The Bible says. . .' was a local occasion, the details of which I do not remember, and the words were probably spoken in the context of a discussion about a very limited subject matter. Over the years, however, that phrase has become the sort of text that invites or conjures up a thousand sermons on the widest range of topics. It is the gate into the field of one kind of authority, but it opens out onto a veritable landscape of controversial matters about authority in general, and how would-be Christians ought to assess it and react to its demands.

The phrase raises vitally important points of issue. The first is concerned with the Church. I have until now used that word as another way of saying the fellowship of believers, but here that will not do. Believers are not just groups of religious people holding common theological tenets. There is within the Christian Church a fundamental belief that Jesus is Lord, and there may be many other Christian beliefs which are as common to Quakers as they are to Methodists or Catholics or Plymouth Brethren. If so, I am bound to add that, even in this ecumenical age, such agreements are still hard to state in anything like a precise way, and certainly the crowd in Hyde Park does not think much of them.

Where then are the guidelines that provide the authority for saying what the true Church is? Are the Methodists sheep or goats? The other matter that follows from the previous chapter is how does the potential believer find the truth about God's existence and purpose, to blend with those other experiences which, although not intellectual, are nonetheless true to life? What are the guidelines that provide the authority to believe in the word? Is the Bible that sufficient and infallible authority? It was in searching for an answer to these questions that I returned to a faith in God which I was able to put in some sort of intellectual order.

To begin then with the Church. There is one answer to the variety of religious beliefs and practices that are found among Christian organizations, and to me it is as simple as it is undubitable. Those who accept the authority of 'the Bible says' are heading for confusion because the Bible says almost everything, and it is not cynical to add that anything you would like to believe, or want to advance or prohibit, can be supported by a text from its pages. There is all the difference between a textbook and a library of the texts. To claim that the Bible is the 'word of God' and is consequently a final and infallible authority has proved in my experience, both in and out of doors, the single most effective deterrent to united churchmanship and successful evangelism.

Historically, those like Calvin were sensible enough to realize that the words, shall we say in the first chapters of the Book of Judges or the last chapters of the Book of Revelation, cannot possibly be acceptable at their face value. So he resorted to the device of declaring a hidden meaning, to what was for the uninitiated an obvious untruth, and by inference making God speak with a 'twisted mouth'. Try that out at Speakers' Corner and you will get the retort I got the other Sunday from a man who said that he didn't think much of a God who seemed to spend most of His time talking in riddles.

The fact is that the Bible is an incomparable servant of the truth but an intolerable master. There is a key with which to open up the door to an understanding of God but that key is not the document itself but what is said in its pages about Jesus Christ, how to see Him against the backcloth of the Hebrew community which was His social inheritance, how to become acquainted with His spirit and teaching, and how to see the effects of His life and witness. The golden thread that binds this library of documents together is the person of Christ. Wholly irrelevant to Him are parts of the Old Testament like the Song of Songs, and the more bloodthirsty records of wars eked out with almost interminable detail as to how the temple was to be furnished, as Chesterton said, by a God whose main attributes were 'a taste in upholstery and a very bad temper'.

To see here and there in the Old Testament prefigurings of the spirit of Jesus as in the great prophets; to read in the New Testament an historical record of his earthly life, as the Gospel writers told the story, and to trace the effects of that life, death and resurrection, the Acts of the Apostles and the Epistles of Paul and others: it is out of this that the authority for the institution of the Church and for its programme can come.

That material had no infallible moral authority of itself, but neither did the Church which inherited it. Hankering after the sort of authority which, in the early days of the Christian era, was as yet unavailable or incomplete, it began to arrogate to itself claims which led eventually to 'the Church says' as the moral equivalent of 'the Bible says' and with the same imprimatur of absolute authority. So strong was the temptation for the Lutheran reformers to avoid the moral problems and dilemmas which the effort to practise the Gospel in the world involved that, when Papal ultramontane authority was repudiated, they found it necessary to put biblical authority in its place. The test of protestant absolute authority was transferred from a person to a document, but its nature was the same. Unfortunately, it does not finally work any better. Indeed, it might be said that, if infallibility is the moral goal for the Church, then a Pope is preferable to a book if only for the reason that a book is likely to be much more garrulous.

In short, there is no such thing as infallibility in human affairs. I am satisfied that it must be proclaimed loud and clear from the Christian pulpit that nothing that is assumed as having been said for us can take the place of that which we are led to say for ourselves. The conciliar government of the Church which tried to find its way by the guidance of the Holy Spirit and is ready to be led, and not dragooned, by that spirit, is the only authority which is primarily a matter of intellectual honesty.

'The Bible says' as a dictum is thoroughly unsatisfactory. Contradictions abound. The only safe way of avoiding this fact is to take the precautions of not reading the script. The records in Kings differ in many instances from records in Chronicles which purport to describe identical happenings. The four Gospel writers give contradictory evidence, particularly in time, of the same events in the life of Jesus. Moses the writer of the Pentateuch describes his own death, and psalms are accredited to authors who in the same time scale could not possibly have written them. Again, the so-called description of the workings of nature with Jesus standing still and

136

donkeys talking, and eclipses taking place at impossible times all combine to justify the assertion that, whatever the merit of the Bible as poetry, biography, vision, and straightforward reporting of the follies of men, it is most assuredly not a statement of eternal and undiluted truth.

Such an indictment in no way undermines the claim that it is by far the most important document in the world, or that sublime heights of insight and creative genius belong to many of its pages and that, if inspiration means anything at all, the language and beauty of what can be found there is unsurpassed. To all such commendation I add that, to me, it is infinitely precious for what it tells me about Jesus, the ideal Son of Man, whom I devotionally worship as the Son of God. For me, therefore, it is an insult to my intelligence to regard every record in the Bible as equal in spiritual value with the high peaks of the Sermon on the Mount or the Twenty-third Psalm.

In fairness, many of the fallacies that the literal approach to biblical authority promotes, are compounded by the way we treat the record as hortatory when it is nothing more than documentary. For example, the story of David and Goliath is almost certainly a piece of folklore reminiscent of an actual event. The dishonesty starts when it is used as a tale with a moral. The first poem I ever recited was hymn no. 316 in the old Methodist Sunday School hymn-book. It began: 'With a shout of bold derision Goliath proudly came . . .' I think that even then I felt a little queasy about the ethics of the story, even as I recited it. I know now that as a cautionary tale it is quite disreputable. Any decent, fair-minded person must have sympathy for Goliath rather than David. It was not a fair fight. Young David with his sling, well out of range of Goliath's sword, had a total of six safe pot-shots at a giant who was unfortunately presenting an unusually large target. Having knocked Goliath unconscious with one of the pebbles from his sling, he chopped off the helpless giant's head.

It is clear to me that to tell the would-be convert to Christianity to read the Bible and accept what he reads as an unquestionable truth, is to invite scepticism and even contempt rather than conviction. I remember a great rally at Kingsway Hall to launch the Christian Socialist Movement in 1960, at which Tony Benn announced the collection and Aneurin Bevan was the principal speaker. I also had something to say and quoted from the Bible in aid of a political point I was endeavouring to make. Afterwards Bevan said that he was unfamiliar with the quotation. I had the impudence to suggest to him that he might pay more attention to the New Testament as a whole. Some time later he told me that he had, in fact, been re-reading the Bible and added: 'Some of what I read was inspiring and appealed to me strongly as it always has done, but you parsons pick out the bits you like and conveniently forget the other bits you don't approve of. What right have you to make a selection from the Bible and where does that right come from?'

That is not a verbatim quotation but the substance is accurate. I can perhaps answer its double-headed challenge by recording my own recovery of an intellectual belief in the Christian faith after the atheistic period of my early student days. For me, it is answer to both aspects of Bevan's challenge and it begins in the very doubt which appears initially as the mortal enemy of faith, but which I came to see as a possibly ally.

I discovered that to doubt the accessibility of a complete and coercive answer to the question 'Does God exist?' is liberating, not frustrating. It may feel painful at the time but to be free from the obsession with a goal of absolute certainty about the universe is a blessing not a curse. It is a healthy condition, for it transfers the enquiry from the mental environment of a book of questions (with a crib at the back which has been torn away), to the environment of a pilgrimage along a road where you may enjoy travelling mercies, although the destination may well be out of reach as yet. It may even be that you find it is better to travel hopefully than to arrive. The all-important consideration is whether the road is open to the traveller. I found that it was. The doubts about the credibility of a supreme being, the doubts as to His goodness, or the doubts as to anything more real than the secular world were the destruction of my juvenile faith, but they could be enlisted as an ally. I had been plagued by the verse of the hymn which declared: 'To doubt would be disloyalty, to falter would be sin'. But now I came to recognize that this was a monumental piece of pious nonsense. The moment I saw it as a good means and not a dead end, I began to apply it to the atheism I had come to accept, and there quickly appeared on my mental screen as many reasons for doubting the atheistic creed as there seemed to be for doubting the theistic one. The arguments which negated a belief in God were not in themselves sufficient to establish the positive belief in His non-existence. Both propositions could be doubted and neither could yield the sort of answer that the proponents of 'The Bible says' attitude confided in. So I read some of the books which argued the Christian faith, of which the incomparably most influential for me was Hans Küng's *Does God Exist?*, not as if they proved their case any more than I now realized that Bury's *History of Rationalism* proved his, but as exercises with doubt. I increasingly found that this discipline, coupled with my personal involvement with those who had resolved their doubts in favour of the Gospel, was yielding a quite positive result. Doubt became the pathway to faith. I found it more reasonable to venture my thinking on a theistic path than on any other and, after half a century of venturing such a faith where there is no pulpit to hide behind and no totalitarian authority to fall back on, I have found this adventure of faith increasingly satisfying.

At the same time, the content of my renewed faith was in many respects different from the sort of belief it replaced. I did not return from the far country of disbelief to the same house which I had been forced to leave. To pursue the analogy, the house to which I returned was by no means fully furnished as the first one had been. The principal rooms were sufficiently equipped to meet my basic needs but quite a number of other rooms were as yet empty.

It was the process of such an intellectual journey that had first driven me away from Christianity until I was able sufficiently to discover a reasonable and ethical substitute and I increasingly found it. Had it not been for the intellectual substitute which I discovered, and to which I have referred here, I cannot believe that I could have remained with the Christian Church from the point at which I found the dogmatism of 'the Bible says' totally unsatisfactory. It was, by the grace of God, here that I found not a substitute but a truth which made the error of that phrase not only insupportable but totally unnecessary. In plain terms, I came back to live on a faith which was much slimmer, its articles fewer and those of which I was certain were surrounded by many other items on the calendar of beliefs where I had to say 'I don't know'. The faith to which I returned included and understood agnosticism as well as a central core of what John Wesley called 'assurance'. This agnosticism was to be a very constant factor in the mission work in London to which I was sent as a raw probationer and which I have pursued now for forty years.

I will select one field of social responsibility for the Christian missioner in which an agnostic condition is to some extent inevitable. The factor broadly indicated by the word 'sex' is an area of human behaviour in which the agnostic approach is the only one that is possible. It is true that the Church has attempted to bring this tumultuous world of sex within a doctrinal framework that is assumed to cover its many manifestations. The initial handicap has been that Jesus said little or nothing about it and St Paul does not seem to have understood the subject at all. The official doctrine of the Church is impeccable in its insistence that the realm of sex must be treated sacramentally. To trivialize it is sinful, and that has been confirmed over and over again in my pastoral ministry. But the besetting sin of theologians throughout the Christian era has been their obsession with a faith once and for all delivered to the saints as both conclusive and complete. There must be no gaps. As a result, the Church has crystallized its teaching about sex only to find that the scientific aspects of this vast subject are not what the fathers of the Church thought them to be. In particular, that basic assumption that man carries the seed of life and that all woman has to do is to cradle it is quite untrue.

Here is the fallacy that is implied in every attempt to use the rule of thumb method on the developing conditions of this human life. It involves the presumption that we already know all the answers. All that is required is to apply the appropriate answer to the particular question. The trouble is that, in this matter of sex, we are now presented with quite new questions that are the product of man's vastly increased capability to interfere with the erstwhile acts of God which were in His hands alone and so beyond our reach. Contraception, abortion, artificial insemination, are all interferences. So are the drugs, and the brain-washing methods which alter personality. So are provisions in modern societies for extra-marital relationships which can take the place of the family unit.

In addition, the irreversible sexual aberrations from the general standards of normalcy, which come under the general umbrella of homosexuality, pose entirely new moral problems when they can be known to be conditions and not perversities. To many of the questions posed by our ever-increasing capacity to interfere with human processes, the agnostic position in the realm of sex as in the realm of the apocalyptic, is the only honest and realistic one.

Nothing is more foolish and unproductive than to give the impression that we Christians are not surprised by any question, that it has already been anticipated on theology. Off-hand, we may not be able to call up the reference number which gives the answer but it is there all right if the questioner will only be patient. The advocate of Christian faith may get away with this in his pulpit, but he can expect short shrift in any public open-air debate.

It reminds me of what is said to have been the response of the Pope when Columbus brought to him a map of the New World. The Pope said that he had known about that New World all the time but had thought it prudent not to say anything. Maybe this is a scandalous misrepresentation of the reaction of the Church to the revolutionary effects of the voyage of Columbus. At least we know that the same Pope recognized that something had to be done and he did it. He drew a line through Columbus' map and declared that all one side of the line was to go to Portugal for the Glory of God and all on the other to Spain for the same eternal purpose. The world might today be a better place in which to live if the subsequent world-wide discoveries of raw materials and economic possibilities had been treated in the same way.

So the belief in God is not a finished product which needs no additions or revisions in the face of a changing society. While it does constitute a number of theological certainties which no circumstance can change, belief is always surrounded by or accompanied by an area of non-belief. Agnosticism about some issues is the constant companion of assurance about others. When I came to terms with the place that agnosticism plays in the make-up of any working faith, I was free from the sense of guilt which had previously assailed me. I now know that compassion (which is a cardinal element in St Paul's commendation of 'charity') is a better guide in some of the ethical puzzles that, to take the area of sexual relations as an example once more, abortion or some methods of contraception propound, than any other principle of judgment.

This agnostic condition must be incorporated in the Christian attitude to a number of problems where to be dogmatic as if the solution was already clear-cut is, to say the least, presumptuous. Agnosticism belongs unavoidably to some questions for which we are basically unequipped with the necessary evidence upon which to come to a conclusion. Doctrines about the next world, eternal life and the ultimate purposes of God's creation, become increasingly unsatisfying as they become more precise. There may be many more things in this amazing universe than our human instruments can detect. We may wonder about a timeless life, we may write poetry about a spaceless experience, or dream of spiritual realities, but to attempt to define timeless, spaceless, immaterial entities (if indeed the word entities is relevant) with the same precision with which we can define a table or a triangle is a delusion.

However, a thorough consideration of this most important philosophical question is beyond my competence, so I must content myself with the effect it has had upon the sort of belief which supplanted and finally banished my atheism. I found a faith which, built upon the evidence that I tried honestly to consider on its merits, prompted me to accept a number of assurances. To accept God as the name for the creator was not only reasonable but persuasive in every way. To believe that God's essential characteristic was love was also a reasonable confidence, though there was a larger element of intellectual dilemma here than in His creative activity. To believe that His creation in love was sufficient to overcome the fact of evil, which I found almost impossible to put into this theological pattern, brought me to Jesus. Once again, trying to weigh the evidence, I found it possible to start with – and increasingly satisfying when I began to practise his presence – thinking of Him as 'the way and the truth and the life'.

As a minister of religion, most of the more academic articles of religion either found their usefulness or their credibility in so far as they became practically effective in describing that way, illuminating that truth, and nourishing that life. In the search for the Kingdom of God as the purpose and quality of His creation, I became less and less interested in the more academic attributes that are attached to the Father and the Son and the Holy Spirit. For example, one lesson which I learned was that, if you can be assured of the humanity of Jesus, His divinity will look after itself. I would add that the acceptance of the agnostic element, which inevitably accompanies belief, has not only eased my own mind but in no way impeded the proclamation of a faith which practises economy as well as confidence. So these are the iron rations rather than the seven-course meal which constitute the nourishment that the would-be Christian can reasonably expect. Theology which offers all the answers is not a suitable diet for those who go on pilgrimage. To be replete is no condition in which to set out on a journey. Saturation of the mind is not the same thing as satisfaction – it clogs it up rather than sets it free.

This is no argument for a permanent fast but an expression of the belief that, in the nature of things, iron rations keep the pilgrim healthy and persistent along a strange but beckoning road. I have found that such a diet of belief, restricted to a few basic foodstuffs, provides a sufficient nourishment for the Christian pilgrimage.

CHAPTER SIXTEEN

THE SHEPHERDS WHO first heard the proclamation which began with 'Glory to God' were in no doubt as to whom the ascription was being made. It was the God of Abraham, Isaac and Jacob who proclaimed His supremacy and commanded total allegience in the first of his Ten Commandments, Thou shalt have no other God before me, with the explicit warning to those who would fall down and worship any other god.

But anyone hearing or overhearing that Advent message today will react differently, and ask himself to what god the message is addressed. The peremptory need to try to answer this question is unavoidable anyhow. Those for whom the Christian faith is approached with a closed mind, and who shut themselves up in a spiritual environment without windows, can apparently ignore the challenge, but let them poke their noses out of doors and they will quickly find that the Christian's God is one among many competitors for the love and heart of men.

Multi-racial societies attract a wide variety of religious cults and, as they develop, present new and hitherto unknown multi-religious problems. I will relate an example of this which, whenever I think of it, intensifies its significance. John Wesley was a fervent believer in and practitioner of open-air preaching. I have tried to follow his example and know something of the hazards and difficulties of this form of evangelism. I am fascinated by what he describes in his journal about his adventures out of doors. He, like most preachers, saw more listeners in the crowd than a head count by an impartial observer would have revealed. The vast numbers to whom he spoke in Gwennap Pit in Cornwall could only have been accommodated there if they had been arranged in layers. I confess that I have been similarly tempted to estimate the size of the crowds in Hyde Park. He and I have both experienced rough handling from time to time, but I have never been threatened with a meat chopper as happened to Wesley in Nottingham. I am well aware of the converting power of his ministry which had such a dynamic effect on eighteenth-century England but, in one respect, his open-air task was easier than that which I have had to face. As far as I am informed, John Wesley was not confronted with the rival claims of other religions. Not so long ago, I was speaking at Hyde Park Corner when I noticed in the crowd a number of shaven heads and saffron robes. Later, I discovered that they belonged to a group of Buddhist missionaries who had been sent over to the West to save, if possible, the British Isles and other European countries from the violence which threatened their very existence. They had begun not improperly in the north of Scotland, were working their way south, and now here they were in Hyde Park. They put their case with great courtesy and equally with great sympathy for our ignorance of the truths which were so evident to them. Not surprisingly, they knew considerably more about Buddlism than I did and they made a deep impression on me and on their hearers.

In that dramatic encounter, the whole realm of religious belief had to be seen against a new backcloth, and there is no honest way of disregarding this modern phenomenon of multi-religious societies in any attempt to assess the meaning and viability of associating Glory to God with the coming of Peace and Goodwill. The subject is vast and I will attempt no more than a number of comments; they certainly spring from my own experience and yield, for me, an optimistic conclusion both for the sustenance of the Christian Gospel and the place it takes in a hopeful future. It is, to begin with, essential to pare down the claims of the Christian so that they do not arrogantly and wrongfully assert a monopoly of truth and goodness. To justify Christianity as if only Christians can be good is utter nonsense.

I will relate another Buddhist occasion. When in Sri Lanka, then called Ceylon, I was taken to the Temple of the Tooth in Kandy where I was shown the tooth of Buddha. He must have been a very large man and I was duly impressed, but what impressed me much more was the Buddhist abbot who was my guide. Even at such short acquaintance, I realized that I was in the presence of a saintly human being, whose goodness was as recognizable as the colour of his robe.

Those who know of the great Islamic saint, El Gazali, would be in no doubt that he was in almost every way as good as St Francis of Assissi, although he offered his goodness to Allah and not to Jesus.

It is surely as impudent as it is inaccurate to claim, as I have read that the evangelist Billy Graham is said to assert, that outside Christianity all was utter darkness.

To denigrate the goodness of those who offer that goodness to other gods, or to no deity at all, is no method of justifying the Christian Gospel and is an aspect of pride which that Gospel calls the greatest of sins. To denigrate the truthfulness of those who find elements of that truth elsewhere than in Holy Scripture, is a contradiction of one of its profoundest statements about the light that lightens every man coming into the world.

Glory to God can be offered to him at many altars and those who worship will do so out of their own background or culture and will contribute something fresh and vital from their prophets and seers. This is not only true to the Hebrew tradition, it is just as true of the Hellenic tradition which figures so prominently in the doctrinal developments in the early Church. There is much validity in the claim that Jesus is the author of the faith, but the book of Christianity contains many chapters written by contributors other than its author, and there is always the need for more editions and further contributions. Did not Jesus himself say: 'More things I have to tell you but you cannot hear them yet'?

Nonetheless, the underlying question remains: can we say that at heart all religions are striving towards the same conclusion and that, beneath the surface of circumstance, they do not contradict one another? Of course we cannot. Most obviously, the Jewish, Christian and Islamic faiths are theistic, the Buddhist faith is atheistic; the Hindu faith is polytheistic; Eastern religions are historically world-renouncing, Western religions largely world-embracing.

While it is true that Glory to God can be proclaimed as the guarantee of Peace on Earth by all sorts of people (who are ethically capable of responding to the love of God) through all kinds of theologically developed critical articulation, there is manifestly no common factor to unite these doctrinal differences. As they stand, they are naturally contradictory in many respects and it is foolish to attempt some kind of theosophy to reconcile these opposites. The history of the theosophical attempt to find a formula that is equally descriptive of all the major world religions, is as *passé* as Madame Blavatsky. There is no highest common factor to be found in all religions beyond 'a vague sense of inoffensiveness and a permanent smile', as Arthur Koestler once put it.

Of all the intellectual difficulties that have dogged my thinking, this is the most intractable. I hold to Christian faith, but that grip is finally an act of the will rather than the finished product of a mental enquiry. Furthermore, I find the arrogance of those who reject the merits of non-Christian faiths deeply offensive, and the defence of Christian theism as the one and final revelation of truth and goodness quite incapable of conclusive proof. Indeed, of all the questions that are asked in the open air and of all the problems facing a person in a multi-racial parish or circuit, this is the one that continues to be most baffling.

I have always been impressed by the negative argument for the Gospel – in the Orthodox Church it is called 'economy'. The supremacy of Christian teaching is not only in what it asserts but, almost as much, in what it leaves out from what other faiths claim for themselves. Aldous Huxley in his *Perennial Philosophy* repeatedly gives evidence of the way the words of Jesus are a distillation of the words of other religious teachers, a selective process rather than an inclusive one. It has been said, for example, that if all the Buddhist sacred documents were to be assembled in one place it would be necessary to put a roofing of canvas over the Grand Canyon to house them. It is true that all the words of the Lord's Prayer can be found in the Old Testament, but it is also pertinent to ask how many more words can be found there that are not in the family prayers and are in conflict with the family spirit. In other words, the Lord's Prayer is almost as significant in what it leaves out from other prayers as to what it includes.

I find the same reaction in contacts with various expressions of Hinduism, which are nowadays much more frequently to be seen and heard in contemporary Western society. One of the objectives, for instance, of the disciples of the Hare Krishna cult is to distribute their literature – and there is so much of it and every guru seems to have a library.

Christianity has been called the religion of the book. Although I cannot accept this as a definition, I value its insistence against a proliferation of ideas and teachings which implies that it is better to put it all in than to leave something out.

This appreciation of the Gospel as a stripped-down version of a wide scope of religious ideas is, I believe, acceptable from another standpoint. The statements that I have made concerning the categorical differences between the great world religions may raise objections. Indeed, such remarks made in open-air debate would inevitably invite the retort that Buddhism or Islam today, for those who really understand, cannot be dismissed in such a cavalier fashion as contradicting one another as well as contradicting the Christian creed. The 'eightfold way' can produce the Buddhist freedom fighter in Cambodia, as well as the final haven from the relentless round of suffering. The Moslem housewife is no longer bound by the visions of the prophet to the degrading subservience of earlier Islamic doctrine. These other faiths are said to be on the move, and so they are.

Among the reasons to account for these changes, there is one which is more important than all the others put together. The basis for its credibility lies in the fact that, in large measure, the faiths of past generations were in conflict. There was little other traffic between them. What, for example, did Christian messengers know of or care about, the more primitive religious cultures of those they endeavoured to convert?

One of the effects of the reduction of the world to the size of a neighbourhood is that there is much more conversation over the garden fence and, whether we like it or not, we are compelled to take notice of one another's domestic habits because most of our houses are terraced or at best semi-detached.

These new contacts have produced two results. Christianity has been examined from Buddhist premises, thus strengthening those elements in the Gospel which are committed to non-violence. Hinduism in its various forms has emphasized spiritual qualities in meditation and bodily activities in the practice of the Kingdom of Heaven. Islam has, particularly in Africa, advocated a racelessness which is fundamental to the wellbeing of the Third World. The Churches in Southern Africa in particular have been challenged by the Islamic revival there to look again at the pentecostal experience of the Apostles by which they proclaimed 'Where there is neither Greek nor Jew, circumcision nor uncircumcision, Barbarian, Scythian, bond nor free: but Christ is all, and in all.' Moreover, if communism is included under the religious umbrella it may be argued that, just as Christianity borrowed from Judaism and Islam from both of them, then communism borrowed from all three. If such a speculation seems to conflict with the contention that only recently has a multi-religious world resulted in an unprecedented interchange of ideas, there are many respects in which all four creeds belong to the same family of world-embracing faiths.

In the recognition of this mingling, if not merging, of religions, I would claim that there are two consequences which can be advanced as going some real distance to justify the Christian claim to primacy. The impact of other faiths on the Christian one has been to stimulate and revive elements in it which were there all the time but were overlaid or prudently forgotten. On the other hand, I think it is fair to say that the impact of Christianity on the non-Christian creeds and practices has been to introduce new concepts that are Christian in essence, rather than to deepen their awareness of their own. When on a recent occasion at Tower Hill, I said that Buddhists did not believe in God, I was roundly denounced as guilty of malicious propaganda. Afterwards I consulted a Buddhist friend of mine who assured me that modern Buddhists have personalized their concept of eternal truth so that nowadays it is perfectly possible for them to hold a theistic position. But where did they get this new idea from? It was surely from the practical demands that flow from a faith which is concerned to win the world rather than escape from it, and that is a theistic requirement.

This process of change seems to follow a selective pattern in the way in which the sacred scriptures of Hinduism, for instance, are subjected to criteria which are built into them but are introduced from outside. The Upanishads are regarded as superior to the more blood-thirsty records of the wars between their deities because they belong to a higher realm of truth, but the records themselves make no such claim. It is a light that comes from outside that enables the reader to distinguish the gold from the base metal. Christianity is the catalyst and the reformations which have taken place in Shinto and Zen, as well as in larger religious bodies, are due largely to the influences that the Christian Gospel has made upon them.

Of course, I realize that I have not painted the full picture, and I have no doubt that some will regard what I have written as both impertinent and grossly unfair. I would plead that at least it can provoke a fellowship of controversy in which I would want to participate, and so would the great majority of kindly critics in the pews and out of doors.

149

I should admit straightaway to two objections that will immediately be raised. I have presented a picture of Christianity by something of the same process of selection which I have applied to these other faiths. But what Christianity have I been describing? For there are many religious organizations professing a wide variety of sometimes mutually exclusive credal and moral doctrines, yet all calling themselves by the name of Jesus. This objection cannot be brushed aside, but the sort of religion that for me represents Christianity at its best can, I am convinced, be seen to run like a golden thread through the so-called Christian era. The saints have called it 'practising the presence of Christ'. It is predominantly the quest for a society called the Kingdom of God. It involves a continuing allegiance to the spirit and teaching of a man called Jesus. When I have used the word 'Christianity', that is what I mean by the word, just as pacifism and socialism represent two of the practical applications of what it means to say 'Jesus is Lord'.

The objection may be that this thread, however accurately it describes my state of mind and outlook, is a minority movement and that I have no right to present it as a universally accepted characteristic either of the Church or of organized Christianity as a fact of history.

The second objection is that what I have said about other world religions is at best that of an observer looking at them from the outside, and such a position is dangerously inadequate where religious matters are involved. It must be accepted that a religion cannot be understood solely on the basis of its intellectual credibility. There is a hymn by Bernard of Clairveaux which says this with a simple certitude in the words: 'the love of Jesus, what it is none but his lovers know' (rephrased as 'none but his loved ones know' in the Methodist hymn-book on which I was brought up, thus investing the words with a spurious propriety while destroying their meaning).

Similarly, the eightfold path can only be recognized by those who are treading it, and it is impossible to assess the merits and messages of the faith of the whirling dervish by simply watching him whirl.

So I will conclude this chapter by stating the position that I have reached after many years, and it is more of a testimony than a final conclusion. For me, the reasons for trying to be Christian are sufficient to outweigh the many difficulties that stand in the way of a final answer, at least in time. The religion in which I was nurtured, and which very imperfectly I have practised, is a belief and an experience that has been a central part of my life, even during my atheistic spasm. I cannot imagine what it would have been like to be born into Zoroastrianism but I would in such circumstances have begun as a disciple of Zoroaster rather than Jesus. I might have been converted to another faith but the sitting tenant in religious matters enjoys much the same advantages as he does in more material affairs.

My spiritual pilgrimage, such as it has been, has confirmed those foundations which my parents laid for me. Jesus is not only the name above every name, but as I have said, He provides me with travelling mercies that include and surpass the guidance that other great religious teachers and prophets have given to the world. It was Charles Lamb who said that, if Plato came into a room, he would rise as a mark of respect, but, if Jesus entered, he would kneel. I am further impressed by the number of great human beings since the time of Jesus who have been proud to be His disciples rather than claiming to be His equal.

The way of life for me is not to exchange the Christian religion for another. Although I am far from satisfied with my response to it, and while I agree that I started with a prejudice in its favour, I proceed with an increasing conviction of its unique veracity. For me, to be a servant of Christ is to be free in almost all else.

I would apply the same reasoning to the Church, but with a somewhat different result. There is only one flock but there are many folds. I have never claimed that the only Christian who belongs to the ecclesiastical fold must be Methodist, although from time to time I have felt compelled to advise sundry members of other denominations not to take unnecessary risks. I should have added that the ethos, where religion is concerned, is not by any means immutable. There is ample room for a Christian liturgy springing not only from the Psalms but from the sacred books of many faiths which could enrich an understanding of the word of God.

In short, there are many introductions to the good news of Peace on Earth and Goodwill Among Men and, if I claim that they are summed up in Jesus and the apostolic teaching of the primitive Church, I gladly recognize that many of them are itemized elsewhere. For those who remain dissatisfied with this defence of Christianity's supremacy, and I can see its imperfections, let me invite them to the fellowship of controversy. Nothing is to be lost and everything is to be gained by the efforts of all believers in religious creeds to outdo one another in goodness. That is the only war which is 'just' and can achieve truth over error and right over wrong.

There is, nevertheless, a postscript which must be added. Some religions are manifestly immoral. The religion of the Borneo head-hunter, for example, is wrong by any natural standard of social ethics. The religion which demanded Suttee is equally to be seen to be morally defective. The religion which cannot distinguish between magic and mystery is out of date in such respects and is no longer credible. Moreover, any religion which requires its adherents to believe things for the good of their souls which are experimentally seen to be untrue, can make no contribution to a thinking faith.

I testify to the deepening conviction that 'natural religion', as distinguishable from 'revealed religion', recognizes certain moral attitudes as absolute. The subject is too large for treatment here but I find it immensely encouraging that in the minds of some of the most distinguished scientists and philosophers of our time, Christianity not only can bear the scrutiny of scientific discovery but thrives on it. Hans Küng has written a definitive thesis on this theme in the book to which I have already referred, *Does God Exist?* I find him unanswerable, not only in his presentation of the basic case for the existence of God, but equally so in his defence of this Christian belief as being the more credible as our general knowledge increases.

That 'natural religion' finds both its source and its application in the Sermon on the Mount, is a discovery or confirmation that is vindicated for me by all my years as a worker priest, if I may claim that title. I am not afraid that Christianity will find itself out of date in the modern world with all its new problems as to how to live the good life. It is still for me that light which is ahead.

152

CHAPTER SEVENTEEN

RECENTLY, I CAME across a card among some old papers and documents of mine. It was signed by a Reverend Edward Weaver, the date was 1914, and it stated that Donald Soper had given his heart to the Lord on a particular Sunday and intended thereafter to abide by this undertaking. I must confess straightaway that, although I remember from those far-off days regular evangelical appeals, I have no clear memory of this particular response, of which that card was the authentification, and I am bound to add that no evidence seems to have survived to indicate any radical changes in my general behaviour around that time which could be attributed to this change of heart.

Yet as I look again at this card, I re-enter a world of religious memories and associations which is in no way impaired or clouded by my failure to recall this example of its power and providence. The axis upon which this world turned was conversion. Everything depended upon conversion. Every effort was required to prosper its aims and all hopes for the future depended upon its achievement. The main responsibility and office of the Church was to preach for conversion, and all the means of grace were to be applied to that end. Missions, special meetings, crusades, services coinciding with the great events of the Christian year, all were intended to reinforce this main thrust of Christian advocacy.

When I remember the advocates of this way of life in my Methodist upbringing and the primary place that conversion occupied in their vocabulary, I am still warmed by the recollection of what really good people they were. I hesitate to use the word 'obsession' to identity this preoccupation with being saved yourself

153

and doing everything possible to get other people saved as well, but from an objective standpoint, obsession it was. The *dévot* was disparaged in comparison with the evangelist. Liturgy had little value except as a stimulus to something more than the cultivation of holiness and therefore even came to be regarded as a form of self-indulgence, for the devout should be seeking the lost rather than cossetting their own souls. Lest anyone should think such an idea a travesty, let him remember that in many a Scottish kirk, everything that went before the sermon was called the 'preliminaries', and in many a Methodist chapel a book of offices was regarded as an impediment to the challenge to flee from the wrath to come.

It could be argued that this preoccupation with conversion has held a much more balanced and integrated place in other denominations, but it remains a matter of observation that the High Church concept of Christianity, which in our day is associated with Anglo-Catholicism and with the increasingly sacramental movements within the Free Churches, is geared to a much more dynamic concern with conversion than previously. Moreover, if the missionary zeal of the eighteenth and nineteenth centuries has somewhat abated, that enthusiasm for the Kingdom of God which began with the offer of God's converting power to the heathen whose life was to be transformed at the point of his baptism into its blessings, is still accepted as the fulfilment of the living injunction to go out 'into the world and make disciples of all the nations'.

The question of conversion is relevant in another area. If Christianity today can be regarded as an umbrella of faith covering all groups who profess a belief in Jesus Christ, then the charismatic groups and the so-called 'sects' are still growing in numbers and influence, especially in South America and the Third World of Africa. When a revival of Christianity is being canvassed, it is among these comparatively novel Assemblies of God and Pentecostal Churches that such a word applies. Only as the spearhead of Christian propaganda does the evidence about conversion justify the confidence that men will offer Glory to God in the Highest, and in consequence achieve and enjoy Peace on Earth and Goodwill among themselves. It is relevant, therefore, to look at the 'conversion' process in detail, as it is to be found in the religious scene today.

The promoting of conversion and its experience as represented in the ministries of John Wesley and George Whitefield have certain elements in common. In both cases, the appeal was set within the option of divine forgiveness and the witness of the spirit of God in a regenerated life or the certain prospect of eternal damnation — fleeing from the wrath to come. This offer was made in simple terms: it required no lengthy build-up or argument, the truth of it was assumed to be self-evident, or perhaps more accurately the need for forgiveness in the face of a consciousness of sin and the menace of eternal punishment needed no arguments to support it. The gift of eternal life, though previously unknown, was not inhibited by doubt when it was offered to the sinner.

The demand for commitment was immediate and the conversion could be as sudden as the concluding words of the evangelist. Those who responded to the appeal experienced all kinds of relief and joy and peace, as Charles Wesley wrote of his own conversion: 'My chains fell off, my heart was free, I rose, went forth and followed Thee.' But frequently that was not the whole story. Such sudden and dramatic conversions were accompanied by physical and psychological phenomena. Some writhed in torment as the devil, according to the onlookers, made his last, despairing attempt to hold on to the sinner before being vanquished by the power of God; some barked like dogs for more obscure reasons. Those who remained tranquil during the conversion experience were a minority. Generally, the response to the Gospel call was stressful, dramatic, and basically emotional in its appearance, although it must be added that the lasting effect for many thus converted was in lives transformed and irreversibly turned in a new direction.

I have described this kind of conversion in some detail for a precise reason. Apart from what can be called primitive human groups, this kind of conversion experience has tended to disappear and to entertain the thought that it will return is quite impractical. Such is my belief, and it is borne out alike by my experience and my attempted analysis of the conditions which have gone to make up its history. I do not imply that the effects of such conversion episodes could not be repeated if they happened today. I simply aver that, for many cogent reasons, to express the hope today that men and women in large numbers will be persuaded to give Glory to God by way of this form of evangelism is fallacious and inoperative. In my entire ministry it has never happened.

Naturally, it may be retorted that the fault was mine but, in its more emotional expression, I do not know any fellow minister in whose ministry it has happened. I have witnessed and taken part over the years in dozens of evangelical campaigns, both in these islands and overseas, and the receptivity of those to whom the invitation to conversion is made, is conditioned by a number of factors that were almost entirely absent in Wesley's day: a smattering of education instead of a grounding in superstition, a familiarity with technology which suggests a secular rather than a spiritual outlook, and perhaps above all a culture which, however imperfect, is built on doubt rather than credulity. To equate the hopes of a permanent revival of religious belief with a revival of this particular conversion practice is, I suggest, futile.

Its avowed success belonged to conditions which, however favourable to this kind of sudden conversion, are in themselves undesirable. They presume ignorance, emotional instability, superstition and they appeal all to often to a moral view of the universe which has more of the characteristics of a tribal god than a heavenly father. Hankering after this sort of approach to conversion is, I repeat, a waste of valuable time, when time in this present age is short. And I submit that the undoubted blessings that come to those who have become morally and spiritually transformed under such methods of presenting the Christian case, have in fact been despite these evangelical blemishes on the face of Christian advocacy.

There is, of course, a form of evangelism which in its quest for immediate conversion does not include or expect the more dramatic psychological accompaniments which belonged to the preaching of this tradition. Moody and Sankey, Torrey and Alexander and, much more recently, Billy Graham, are names in the English-speaking world which call to mind a challenge to conversion which does not depend so much either on a degree of ignorance and superstition, or a fear of hell.

I am able to look back on more than fifty years of ministry and, if I ask myself what has been my ambition in all aspects of that ministry, the answer is unmistakable. I looked for success, to see the conditions of life for those to whom I was to minister, to see the Old Kent Road and the streets of Islington and West London look more like the Kingdom of God, but that general ambition depended for any practical outcome on two objectives, both of which were concerned with individual people rather than society as a whole. One was to mobilize an effective group with whom we could

156

maintain the work and witness of the Church, the other was to win recruits so that such work and witness might grow. I therefore ask myself what part in this enterprise has been played by my more domestic efforts at recruitment and mobilization, and how has the wider evangelical effort to convert men and women affected my particular activities?

The honest answer is that the number of sudden conversions has been as minimal in regard to this more modern form of conversion appeal as it has been totally absent from the more traditional one. Neither home-grown nor imported products of this pattern of evangelical appeal have made any significant contribution to the prophesied time of Peace and Goodwill in the churchmanship in which I have been continuously involved. Then is conversion itself to be written off in this bleak story? I believe not. To look even more closely at the failure of the two sorts of mass evangelism that I have tried to describe, is to understand all the better the genuine marks of real conversion to Christianity and to find reassurance in their validity.

What actually happens at a Billy Graham campaign? I have no wish to asperse the sincerity of those who promote and undertake it and I am not concerned at the moment with the theological and Biblical foundation upon which it is reared. The permanent effects, however, have not been a perceptible increase in the numbers of registered believers either here or across the Atlantic. How is this irrefutable statistic to be reconciled with the figures that express the response to the appeal to stand up and be counted – the thousands who decide for Christ on the spot, so to say? The first answer is that getting converted is, for some devout members of Christian bodies, almost an occupational requirement. They find it much easier to live a kind of cradle life than to grow up.

The challenge of growing up into Christ is easy enough to proclaim from the pulpit with all its instructions and demands. I can think of so many harassed mothers in the mothers' meetings of city missions for whom the lofty injunction to practise the life of commitment to spiritual things is little short of callous impertinence. No wonder the simple demands of the cradle provide a sort of compensation for the intolerable difficulties that leaving that cradle present. An evangelical campaign identified with Christian beginnings is a most welcome relief from tension and frustration. It is as good as a spring holiday.

157

Nevertheless, to count these revivalists as new recruits is quite misleading. From the first Billy Graham campaign in 1954, the names of five so-called converts from Harringay were passed on to us in the West London Mission. Three of them had been members with us for years and, of the other two, one replied when we wrote to him that there must have been a mistake, and the other could not be traced.

The experience of fellow ministers was much the same. When from the total number of converts is subtracted those who stood up *'pour encourager les autres'*, those who came out upon the impulse to see what it was like, and those who were swept off their feet by the emotions created by nostalgic hymns and long-forgotten childhood days within the framework of the Church, what remains? A very small number of people, young and old, for whom those occasions triggered off a religious process which needed such moments to bring a developing spiritual condition to ignite it. This form of evangelicism provided the occasion of conversion not its cause.

Finally, this method of appeal for sudden conversion is being recognized by those who activate it as obeying the law of diminishing returns. After all, hell is no longer a future certainty, but for the Grace of God, and the sense of personal sinfulness is by no means as potent as it was – its weight is nothing like the burden the Christian bore on his back as he left the city of destruction. To rest the hopes of the Gospel on repeated campaigns soliciting this form of response, is to find those hopes less and less likely to be widely attained and, what is even more serious, the tares in this field choke the wheat. Justifiably or not, the sort of Christian propaganda which centres on the surrender to Christ as an immediate requirement at the end of an evangelical appeal within the framework of an evening's hymns and prayers, is often treated with the contempt which it may not deserve but increasingly attracts. At Speakers' Corner, in particular, it is an embarrassment. In general, it no longer works.

Then must the Christian advocates look elsewhere for the opportunistic weapons with which to fight the good fight? Not at all. The Christian life begins in a response of the will to the promptings of the heart and mind. A man or woman may entertain the warmest appreciation of the character and spirit of Jesus and yet do little or nothing about it. I know scores of such people but they are not Christians and will tell you so as if such inactivity is a virtue.

Let me quote an example. One of the finest brains I have known belonged to the refugee Paul Winter, whose family perished in Auschwitz and whom I encountered in rags and misery in Hyde Park. Broken by suffering of many kinds, he kept himself alive by applying his mind to an examination of the 'Trial of Jesus'. He wrote a book with that title which is already a classic and as Jew became a master of Christian theology. He never became a practising Christian.

The emphasis on conversion is absolutely central to membership of the Christian community. The feeling of love does not become Goodwill on fire until it is activated by the will. Faith only becomes the power of God unto salvation when the will transforms it into trust.

So when I look again at that decision card from my early youth, it does much more than attract the objections and criticisms which I have listed. I am reinforced from many aspects of the Christian ministry in the conviction that bad conversion strategy must not be allowed to turn out the good, and I am emboldened to set down some conditions that this imperative part of offering Glory to God in the Highest must observe.

The first of these conditions is that the appeal for a wilful response to the evangelical invitation must take into account the various mental and physical stages of development in the congregation that receives such an appeal. To lump together a crowd of young and old, members of differing cultural groups or of none, the anxious and the complacent, as if the same presentation of the Gospel will meet all of them where they are, and persuade them to go where the Gospel directs them, is morally and intellectually untenable. The apparent success of such coagulation is found, according to the psychologist Adler, in the one response that can be evolved from such a bundle of humanity: that it is a mass reaction which has nothing to do with a conversion experience.

Again, most campaigns that for one reason or another attract large crowds, ask too much and ask for it too soon. A half-hour's warming-up period, then another half-hour's exhortation, taking for granted an entire set of ideas and assumptions, which is then immediately followed by a high-pressure demand for a total commitment, breaks the canons of intellectual respect and moral dignity. I believe it to be a form of totalitarianism in religious matters just as dangerous as fascism is in the political realm. It is a

159

form of fascism in its disregard of the rights that belong to a person's own thoughts. It burns the books instead of inviting its hearers to read them.

The alternative to this conversion by hosepipe is the tailoring of the evangelistic message to the conditions of the hearer and, consequently, the appeal to the will of the hearer to make the kind of response which is fitting. I will illustrate. I was invited, while doing some work with the Free Churches in Japan, to address in Hokkaido a group of students who, by their questioning through an interpreter, I could tell were largely unaware of Christianity either as a culture or a theology. The one thing that I felt I could decently ask of my hearers was for them to make up their minds that they would continue to listen to the Christian case. More than that would have been impertinent; less, a failure in vocational opportunity. I have no subsequent evidence as to the result following this address but the Japanese minister who organized the occasion wrote to me some time ago that, from that day, there had been created and continued a fellowship of those who in fact did set out to understand the Christian case. He went on to say that he thought it not wrong to liken this response to the initial response hundreds of years ago to those Jesuit missionaries in Japan who, in many cases, reported back to their European authorities that they had very little success, only for their successors to find that when Japan was opened up in the nineteenth century to Western influences again, some of these discussion groups had persisted over all the years.

I hope that the call to conversion to which I must have responded as a young boy was couched in language which a child could understand, although I suspect that I complied, so as not to be left out. After all, to ask a child to give himself heart and soul to Jesus is almost meaningless. Much better to invite him or her to come to the common table with his parents, and so to become part of the life of the Church while its larger responsibilities are still far beyond his comprehension.

There are many ways of response to Christian discipleship. It all depends where you are when the challenge is made and, unless the challenger meets the possible pilgrim at his point of departure, it is most doubtful whether he will be able to speed him on his way. Even then the evangelist must be patient. There is a kind of courtesy which has accompanied the religious activities of the great saints and that is why St Francis of Assissi is the best loved of all.

I have found in preaching for conversion that there is everything to be said for dogged persistence. I know that sometimes the opportunity once missed may not recur and that every sermon in every service, and every corporate act of worship from Holy Communion to singing chorus hymns, should be a vehicle for decisions. But where I have seen real and permanent changes in the lives of those with whom I have been in contact, and those changes have been Christ-like, they have been the product of a series of decisions over a period of time. I will go further. Where those changes have had anything to do with me, they owe more to a consistent and continuing witness, patiently unfolded and reflecting an understanding as best I could achieve of the individual person.

Wet or fine, I have made it a rule to go to Tower Hill every week whether the crowd and the hecklers were likely to be there or not. Sunday by Sunday, I have presided at morning and evening public worship for any who cared to be present, and I have preached the Gospel as the answer to the day by day problems of the congregation. I am satisfied, not with my performance, but that, despite its grievous imperfection, this continuity of evangelism and the consistency in which I have endeavoured to carry it out over the years has done more to encourage those to whom I have tried to minister to take the appropriate steps to a Christian life than all my specific sermons and exhortations put together.

From this experience I draw the confidence that the offering of Glory to God is no vain hope. The more you stick to it, the better your arguments, and the more likely that those who hear them will make an optimistic response.

CHAPTER EIGHTEEN

THE EVANSTON CONFERENCE of the World Council of Churches was held in America in 1954. At the time, it was hoped that the Russian Orthodox Church would send a representative. However, one would only be sent if the Patriarch agreed and, as the Conference drew near, there was evidence that the Patriarch was against the idea. It was decided, therefore, to endeavour to suggest to him that it could be in the best interests of his own Church as well as for the well-being of the Council if he would reconsider the matter.

The Reverend Dr Charles Raven accordingly took a small group of British churchmen to Moscow to suggest to His Holiness that he really should appoint somebody to go Evanston. I was a member of that group. It was not an easy task because there was some difficulty in proposing to a patriarch that he should have second thoughts – it was rather like advising God to think again. However, the mission was successful and the Russian Church was represented.

I remember the trip for many reasons quite apart from its principal objective. It afforded a fascinating opportunity of seeing how a Church can live in a society wherein it is officially labelled as a superstitious institution. One incident stands out in my memory above all others, and to recount it opens up an area of Christian living which cannot be excluded from this question of the validity of the claim that Peace and Goodwill are contingent upon the profession of faith.

Speaking no Russian, we took along with us a young Cambridge graduate who was fluent in that language. In addition, the Patriarch assigned to us a Russian priest whose English was impeccable. I came to know the priest quite well and was able, towards the end of the visit, to ask him a number of questions which I felt sure he would answer rather than evade. I asked him what it was really like to profess a faith denounced as superstition in an environment where evangelism is proscribed through worship is permitted. I shall never forget the beginning of his answer. He said: 'I have to recite ten "Our Fathers" before I can even begin to pursue my vocation as a priest.' He then went on to explain the difficulties involved in public worship which, strangely enough, he regarded as posing a greater problem than that of evangelism which, unlike worship, was actually forbidden. It was, however, a shock to a non-conformist like myself to think of the Lord's Prayer as a doorway to the devotional life, like a telling of the beads or the use of a rosary. Now, as I look back, it has opened up a window not only onto the vicissitudes of religion in the Soviet Union but to the wider panorama of worship as one of the ingredients of religion itself.

Until now I have commented upon the first words of the Christmas message in terms of its credibility as a belief, but to the shepherds who first heard this introduction to the good news, it was much more an acclamation than a credal statement. That Russian priest had learned the hard way how essential for the practice of the Christian life is the worship of the would-be believer. Worship is the soil, or one necessary ingredient of it, in which faith and works grow. There, in a soil which contained none of the elements of worship and none of its intimations, he was hard put to prevent his spiritual life from withering. The ten Our Fathers were his almost desperate attempt to recover the environment which religion absolutely requires and without which it cannot breathe. His remark, which first repelled me as the quite imperfect use of a prayer, became the spur to a developing realization of something which I had almost taken for granted.

I have lived my life in surroundings saturated with religious associations. This is not to say that Britain is a worshipping community but instead that those who are inclined to worship here find themselves at home rather than in a foreign land such as that which surrounds the Russian priest. I am here less concerned with those born into a religious family and who themselves follow in the parental footsteps, but with the sort of people with whom I was thrown into early contact in the West London Mission. Most of them, as I have said, knew the name of the church they stayed away from. Most of them had been to church on three significant occasions in their lives: christenings, marriages and funerals. Having officiated at hundreds of such occasions, I well realize that, in the first and second of these events, the principal participants are not fully conscious and in the third event, of course, they are not conscious at all!

But here again is the spiritual variation of the assertion that the onlooker sees most of the game. The congregations at these ceremonies are doing something that comes naturally. The same background to worship belongs to the public life: the mayor is himself worshipped and equipped with a chaplain; civic festivals are still associated with the Christian year; football matches are accompanied by the singing of 'Abide With Me', although surely that is the most unsuitable choice of words for such occasions; sessions of Parliament begin with prayers – as someone once said, the chaplain looks at the Members and prays for his country. Some holidays still coincide with events in the life of Jesus.

If all this falls far short of public life that is demonstrably Christian, it has all the more significance in as much as our culture provides the same background to worship, though not so formally as in these examples. No great city is without its cathedral, no village without its church and its chapel; no library is without a majority of books which directly or indirectly reflect Christian culture, no school without vocational or obligatory religious instruction; and, indeed, there is no intelligent conversation which does not depend heavily on words and phrases from the Bible.

Looking back on the successes and failures that have attended the evangelical efforts in which I have been engaged, I have not been compelled to create a religious background before I could begin. It was already there. How different it would have been to face, as an Orthodox priest has to do, a communist environment.

Some years after the Moscow visit, another experience reinforced my conviction that we clergy in the West need to examine much more seriously the vital relationship of religion and churchmanship to the prevailing favourable or hostile political and social climate. I was invited to visit the Methodist Church in Poland. There I found a broken, divided Church with some indubitable saints, oppressed with the full force of opposition from the State and enjoying none of the concessions which the dominant Catholic community was able to squeeze out of the communist government. This was most cruelly the case in Nova Huta a city which, as its name suggests, was completely new. Provision had been made for the Catholic faithful to worship in an old church some miles away, but no concession whatsoever was made to the other Christian groups. Further, for impenetrable reasons of State security, the Catholics were regarded by the government as patriots, whereas the Methodists were branded as traitors.

Nova Huta appeared to me to be secular in the exact sense of the word, and I wondered how many Our Fathers or Wesley's hymns I would have needed to recite or sing in order to keep my faith alive. I have often considered since that visit whether, in such an environment, my only hope would have been with a Roman psalter rather than a Methodist hymn-book. Although I have never been confronted with such a dilemma, the experiences I have related serve to establish that intimate relationship between God as the object of devotion in a congenial atmosphere and God as the object of obedience in relation to ultimate reality.

To insist that *'laborare est orare'* is correct, but the reverse – to praise is to work – is just as true. An atmosphere congenial to worship is already present in the societies of the West: it is there to be used. Such an atmosphere is largely absent now in the predominantly secular societies which can generally be called Marxist. Therefore it has to be created, and the courage and perseverance of such 'creators of worship' is a glorious entry in the contemporary history book.

In this country 'Glory to God in the Highest' has been declared against the backcloth of an almost universal belief in God. It was announced to a group dominated by ideas and emotions that were theological even before they were practical. God was already there to be glorified. Since then the fervour or certainty of belief in the Deity has varied, theological priorities have tended to lose caste but, until recently in the West, to give God Glory for His promise of Peace and Goodwill was the natural inference to be drawn, as well as the natural premise to be accepted. With the emergence of the totally secular state, however, all this has changed for the first time in recorded history. Whether that change is likely to be permanent is a fascinating speculation and there seems to be increasing evidence that turning out religion by the front door is an open invitation to it to enter by the back. While I believe this to be the case, it is too early to regard such a process as axiomatic.

What does emerge from the 'ten Our Fathers' incident is the great

165

peril that religion has to face when the religious environment no longer exists and, in those societies where it does still exist, the question must be asked: what is happening to the marks and reminders of Christianity which have provided the soil for worship? Upon the answer to that question depends the divine authority for belief in the future well-being of God's children, for there can be no doubt that there has been a widespread erosion of the sort of background which I have described.

The example that communist regimes present may not be repeated in our society, but the dire threat which such examples pose cannot be shrugged off. The fact is that their complete secularization is not entirely attributable to Marxian dogma. They reflect important social aspects endemic to the modern world. I will attempt to list some of them.

Firstly, the urbanization of developed human groups is itself a disincentive to the sort of social life which makes the potential believer feel at home. Life lived in rural conditions (and until recently town life was not cut off from rural aspects) was never far from the natural world. The more people live in great conurbations, the less vital and the more artificial is their contact with basic values. Light which has to do with the rising and setting of the mysterious globe called the sun, becomes a commodity obtained by pressing a switch. Summer heat and winter cold, which once obeyed laws that appeared capricious if not mysterious, become everyday conditions regulated by domestic machinery. Above all, perhaps, exposure to the world of nature, though it does not of itself recommend God's goodness and though it has all too often stimulated superstition, has emphasized man's dependence. But the artificial world of a tower block tends to destroy this sense of dependence and in its place there is a self-sufficiency which every new so-called 'conquest' of nature invites. Alongside the effect of the secularized life, has developed a secular intellectual life just as repulsive to the familiarity of a religious culture.

I can best put this point in the form of a conversation I had with Dr Ernest Rattenbury, one of the great Methodist preachers, just before he died. Dr Rattenbury was one of my predecessors in the West London Mission. He had conducted crowded services in the Aldwych Theatre when Kingsway Hall was being built in 1913 during the general reconstruction of Kingsway itself. I asked him what was the main difference between the congregations of those

166

pre-First World War days and those to which he was still preaching in his ninetieth year. He answered that, when he began his ministry, he could count on a general sense of guilt in the congregation. Now it was a general sense of doubt.

Broadly speaking, my experience would confirm the second part of that observation, but that doubt is not so much the finished product of an intellectual process as a predisposition to question rather than to accept. The proof of the religious pudding is not so much in the eating of it as in the correctness of the ingredients and the cooking of them.

My beloved mother, in her lifelong commitment to education, claimed that the emphasis when she began teaching was on the accurate translation of the Latin word, '*educare*', to nourish with food. In her later years, the other Latin word, '*educere*', the drawing out into clear relief of what was already there, was preferred, and one of the dominant elements in that educative process was the tendency to criticize what was offered. My own experience bears out that very important transfer of emphasis. Whereas not so long ago religious life was the product of rowing with the tide, the situation today is at least that of slack water and more often of rowing against the tide.

Perhaps the most startling example of the non-religious background to so much of contemporary life is to be found in the 'Death of God' argument. This does not start in atheism. God was there to begin with but He has now ceased to exist because He is worn out, the work He once undertook is now farmed out elsewhere and, in a condition of total unemployment, He has lost the will to live. I remember how I reacted to this extraordinary thesis when visiting the United States a year or two ago. I was confronted with a reporter who, without preliminaries, asked me bluntly: 'Is God dead?' I answered that I hadn't heard he was unwell.

It was not just a flippancy. My entire being — spiritual, moral, political, philosophical — is composed of one assurance. There is nothing wrong with God. The trouble is with His family. The sickness 'even unto death' is in us, not in Him. To ask about the health and even the existence of God was preposterous to me and still is. Yet the 'ten our Fathers' incident has served as a constant reminder that, in the Christian race, I had the inside track, compared not only with those who had to run that race under the enormous handicap of a hostile environment but compared with a generation in which religion was not condemned but increasingly

167

ignored. The growing secularization of our modern society presents increasing difficulties to the practising Christian. The passing of almost every year in Hyde Park and on Tower Hill raises perhaps more acutely the problem of preaching the Gospel when you are using a language which has more or less become dead or is no longer current.

So how is faith to be generated today when it is not sown in a field already ploughed and ready at least to receive it? The answer must be that the field has to be ploughed before the seed can be sown with any likelihood of its germinating. It has often been claimed that there is no salvation outside the Church. This was the kind of intolerance that, as a non-conformist, I rejected and the more rigid the claims of particular Churches, the more I reacted against it. But what if the meaning of that assertion is that there is no salvation which is not a plant of faith living and growing in a soil of fellowship? The real import of the comments in this chapter confirm irresistibly to me that giving Glory to God is not a solo from however sublime an archangel but an anthem for all parts to be sung by a choir. I do not know how many choristers took part in the first rendering of that anthem, but I have no doubt that the shepherds heard it as a concerted effort, indeed as a concert, for such it was.

It is with this great truth in mind that I end with a personal testimony. The worshipping community is the only sufficient base from which the Christian can proceed with his evangelism and his good works. It is one thing to convince a questioner in the open air that he has got his priorities wrong or to persuade him that he needs to do something about his sins or his problems, but it is quite another to represent those priorities to him in action or to give him the practical evidence of his sins forgiven and faith revived. A communion service in my ministry has proved a much more powerful argument than a cosmological one, not least because it involves those other sides of our human make-up that mere intelligence cannot reach.

But how to set up that communion in the first instance? John Wesley found the answer. Lenin, with obvious modifications, borrowed it. And they were both residuary legatees of the gift of Pentecost, although one of them was probably unaware of his sources. It is the cell structure of growth. Wesley developed it in the Methodist class meeting, Lenin in the communist cell, and the Acts of the Apostles sets out the 'praxis' which both of them followed towards their different ends. This call to the Christian and the world for action, to convert to Christianity, is not the same as a Sunday morning service in the parish church or the 'hymn-sermon sandwich' still beloved by many free churchmen. It is a dynamic fellowship of those who are already committed to the cause in which they meet. It is deliberately small in number in order to deepen that fellowship and not dilute it. It is mutually interrogatory. Members of those first class meetings not only shared their experiences, they also put one another under test.

The Chinese Communist cell apparently practises such self-examination within the attending group. It contains acts of worship or of devotion to accepted doctrines. These are invariable and therefore, unlike what is called free prayer, can be anticipated. Similarly, it is a great mistake to think that the prayers in the great days of the Methodist class meetings wandered all over the globe, as I have known them to do all too often in longer acts of worship. The reiteration of the accepted themes of spiritual or secular salvation maintains a thread of certainty. You know where you are or, perhaps more accurately, where you ought to be.

In one sense the Methodist class meeting was very largely an early Methodist experience, and in certain detail it is unrepeatable. It was the coming together of fervent Methodists in small groups of not more than eight people and, in this devotional atmosphere of mutual confession and belief, was a great reinforcement of their faith. At the same time, the reappearance quite recently of what are called house churches is an indication of the way in which the more general and public occasions of Christian worship tend to be accompanied by more personal and intimate meetings of the faithful. Here lies one of the very important elements in any optimism about the maintenance of churchmanship in the contemporary situation.

I would not pretend that this cell structure as the sufficient environment for a religious faith and practice is not, like everything else in this temporal world, liable to change and decay. Yet as I think hopefully of the future, everything that belongs to that optimism hinges upon a revival of the faith in which the blessing of peace and the tranquillity of social harmony are realizable because they are inherent. Immense rallies for peace or justice, crowded services, mass evangelistic occasions, are likely to be less effective today than the infiltration of our present divided society by tiny cells of devotees which 'proliferate before they endeavour to coagulate', as one delightful Quaker put it to me the other Sunday. This is the kind of Church which can offer Glory to God, and I will presume to add that the Quakers in their silences have discovered the profound secret that God is both incomprehensible and accessible. It is the spirit of Jesus that unites those who are more concerned to walk in His steps than to define His being: but that is no bar to worship which remains the driving force of all that such worshippers do and seek to be. As the negro preacher said, worship enables the worshipper to 'unscrew the inscrutable'.

To set such an example as this sort of cellular religious life provides, in no way displaces denominational allegiances and public acts in celebration of the faith. The coming together in small groups of worshippers from all the Churches is the highroad to unity. More importantly, it is the means of recovery of pure religion in the soil of natural religion and I see increasing signs that this is what is happening or beginning to happen. There is no salvation outside the Church but only if that historic institution becomes a living fellowship for today's world.

POSTSCRIPT

I BEGAN THIS 'autobiographical inquiry' by making use of the method adopted by Marcel Proust in his tremendous work *A la Recherche du Temps Perdu* of using particular remembered occasions and incidents as the gate into the field of past experience. I conclude by using his conclusions derived from such research as compared with those to which I have come. There is a radical difference between the two.

For Marcel Proust, the conclusion to which he felt impelled as the outcome of study of lost and recovered time, was that time is the great destroyer. Nothing, or nearly nothing, is impervious to its malignant influence – love is killed by jealousy, innocence succumbs to corruption. In this almost universal carnage, only art is not destroyed by time.

While its moral base is substantially different from the Christian outlook, Proust's emphasis on the transience and the 'change and decay' which belong to time is echoed in many of the hymns we sing:

> *Time, like an ever-rolling stream,*
> *Bears all its sons away;*
> *They fly forgotten, as a dream*
> *Dies at the opening day.*

In writing this book, I have found that the kind of statement which is exemplified by these lines from a Hebrew psalm, translated by Isaac Watts, cannot be ignored. They demand attention because they are inseparable from the grim facts and inevitable doubts that are

171

part of life as I have come to experience it. I have never found it possible to read off, so to say, from my own experience a conclusion that 'There is a book (the book of experience), who runs may read which heavenly truth imparts', or that 'God is good all nature says'. Others may rejoice to sing, 'If our love were but more simple we should take Him at His word and our lives would be all sunshine in the sweetness of our Lord', but that is not my experience and I am not sure I want it.

Nevertheless for me, the Christian call is a call for action here and now. Obedience to that call yields the increasing certainty of its eternal truth and power.

What I can say is that, like Proust, I have tried to remember times past and not in the first place to overlay them with contemporary attitudes, but to see those contemporary attitudes within their historical perspective.

Despite the ravages of time, and the limitations it sets to our fuller understanding of matter and space, I am today the more confident than ever that the song of the Heavenly Host is the half-hidden meaning behind our human experience. They belong to the City of God and, as Carlyle wrote, the City of God remaineth.